w.

I HOPE now you weren
on last night.... I'm gl
steering clear of

l get me
ere?

her feet. Poor thing.   He's cracked. Away. With. The fairies.

nket on again
d it nearly May.   Will you have it in a bowl
ng my eye.   or with a wafer?

I suppose you play this 'Angry Birds' too do you? . . .
On your computer is it? . . . On your PHONE?!

n't know WHERE the week went to.

me? Stop   Have you everything now? ...Are you SURE?
ou.   . You always leave something here after you.

t another wear out of that.

redit for 0 8 7, please, and I
atting it on the phone for me   I've nothing only Rich Tea.
ood lad?   They'll have to do ye.

hts are drawing in.   You've grand curls godblessyou.

You needn't think now, Wasp, that you're getting any of this bun.

our new school trousers
the name of God did you   No we didn't hear a THING
anage that?   about it. But of course she
                                                  tells us NOTHING.
pe their feet on the way in?

And it didn't do us a BIT of harm.

ou might as well be talking to the wall.

Bucketing.

Isn't it well for ye?

the book of
Irish Mammies

Marie,

*To an Irish Mammy
from an Irish Mammy,*

Love A R.

12 · 12 · 13

COLM O'REGAN

TRANSWORLD IRELAND

TRANSWORLD IRELAND
an imprint of The Random House Group Limited
20 Vauxhall Bridge Road, London SW1V 2SA
www.transworldbooks.co.uk

First published in 2012 by Transworld Ireland,
a division of Transworld Publishers

Design by Nick Avery
Illustrations by Doug Ferris
Photograph on page 83 © Photocall Ireland

A CIP catalogue record for this book
is available from the British Library.

ISBN 9781848271487

Addresses for Random House Group Ltd companies outside the UK
can be found at: www.randomhouse.co.uk
The Random House Group Ltd Reg. No. 954009

The Random House Group Limited supports the Forest Stewardship Council
(FSC®), the leading international forest-certification organization. Our books
carrying the FSC label are printed on FSC®-certified paper. FSC is the only
forest-certification scheme endorsed by the leading environmental organizations,
including Greenpeace. Our paper procurement policy can be found at
www.randomhouse.co.uk/environment

Printed and bound in Great Britain by
Clays Ltd, Bungay, Suffolk

6 8 10 9 7 5

MIX
Paper from
responsible sources
FSC® C016897

Contents

Introduction

This book is a celebration of the phenomenon of the Irish Mammy.

It started life as a Twitter account called @irishmammies. If you don't know what Twitter is, don't worry; that's not what this book is about. One way to describe Twitter is as the online equivalent of graffiti on the wall alongside a fairly busy secondary road. If you've time you'll see it, but if you're not on that road you'll never see it. And you won't miss much.

I set up a Twitter account to relay some of the things that Irish Mammies say. They're not necessarily words of wisdom — just words of living from my own mother and other mothers I have witnessed in action. Within hours of the account's inception, these little snippets — 140 letters or fewer in length — were being re-tweeted (the Twitter equivalent of he-said-she-said) around the place. Over the course of the next few months, thousands of people started to follow @irishmammies. ('Follow' is Twitter parlance for 'sign up to read what she has to say'. There's nothing messianic going on here.)

Across the world, emigrants thinking of their own Mammies at home, people who had met an Irish Mammy and others who suspected they were turning into one latched on to the @irishmammies Twitter account and became very fond of her.

So now there's a book.

It's not the first exploration of the Irish Mammy and neither will it be the last but, hopefully, it's an enjoyable one.

Not everything the Irish Mammy says and does in this book will mean all things to everyone. There are of course many different types of Irish Mammy, but whatever the variations are, you'll recognize some things. This is a woman who more than likely will have spent some time on a small, rainy island in the Atlantic, with the nights drawing in, worrying about damp clothes and unaired beds, feeling the lift from a stretch in the evenings, making and drinking gallons of tea with neighbours and family (being sure to scald the teapot), ordering children down off a wall for fear they'd break their neck, being surprised by prawn cocktail, and having the pavlova.

She has re-addressed countless letters to a variety of locations around the world. She knows far more than her children give her credit for and often wonders what's keeping them at all.

Now she's in a book, so call in if you're passing, but be sure to ring ahead.

Colm O'Regan

A Word from Irish Mammy

When he said he was doing a book, I got an awful land. You know, he had a good job, a degree and all, and he threw it all up to go into I-suppose-you'd-call-it the entertainment business, but sure anyway all we can do is support him. As long as he's happy, that's the main thing. But isn't it fierce hard for the young people now? I don't know where they're all going to get jobs, the-Lord-save-us.

He gave it to me to read and I flicked through it all right, but I haven't had time to read it in detail, to tell you the truth. We've been very busy: Himself with his hip, and then we're both booked in to have our teeth cleaned tomorrow, so I don't know when I'll get a chance.

The bit of it I saw seemed grand, though I don't know are some bits an exaggeration? But sure there's always going to be a bit of exaggeration in these things for the entertainment value, I suppose.

Then, would you believe, didn't the publishers say to me, 'Mammy, have you any words of wisdom at all for the readers?' Well, I wouldn't say I'm that wise now indeed. We all muddle through the best we can and there's far wiser than me around.

But whatever ye do, let ye bring the coat anyway. If it's too warm ye can take it off, but it'd be handy to have. You could get an awful cold this time of the year.

Mammy

I

The Making of Her

She didn't lick it up off the stones.

The Mammy we know and love didn't just happen. She is the product of her origins and influences. But what are those origins?

Archaeological evidence is frustratingly rare, but in what little there is we can see some familiar depictions, as in this cave painting of a hot press in Altamira, which shows that the Irish Mammy's eternal fear of damp was at the centre of prehistoric life.

The ancient Irish Ogham script was believed to have originally been a representation of a washing line with clothes-pegs and was used by Irish Mammies to communicate drying conditions.

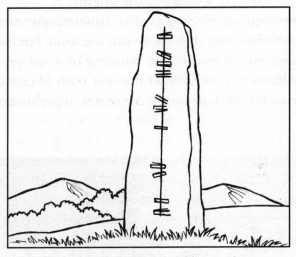

Translates as: 'A grand bit of drying out'

You couldn't believe half of it – the Irish Mammy in mythology

As is often the case where there is a lack of hard historical fact, the missing details are filled in by myth. There are competing theories of the origin of the Irish Mammy. Some say she is descended from

Cessair, granddaughter of Noah, who was said to be the first woman to arrive in Ireland. This would make sense, as Mammy would always have had relatives in the Missions. The Fir Bolg — so named because they ate too quickly and got pains in their stomachs — came from Greece, but they seem unlikely ancestors, as Irish Mammy for some reason could *never* get any colour on the back of her legs. The Tuatha De Danann — the ancestors of traditional music groups — may also be a progenitor, but although Mammy was 'kinda musical' she never joined a band. That leaves the Milesians — descendants of a daughter of an Egyptian pharaoh. While Mammy would love a cruise, she would never be foolish enough to get involved in any pyramid schemes.

Or could the answer be found somewhere even more mysterious? Could Irish Mammies be the surviving rulers of the lost continent of Atlantis? Atlantis was said to be an idyllic land where peace reigned and the superior intellect and capability of the people had all but eliminated danger. This angered the gods of Atlantis, who, slighted by the fact that the people were 'gone too lackadaisical altogether', rained fire and flood upon the land. Some stories say that all were destroyed, but a little-quoted passage in the writings of Greek geographer Strabo hints there might have been survivors:

And lo! The Atlantean sky and land both torn in two
And all were gone save one small boat with precious cargo.
Women, brave and indomitable,
Tissues in their sleeves just in case.
They sailed east into unknown dangers
And cried in one voice,
'Didn't I say this would happen?
Wouldn't you want to be fierce careful.'

And thus Irish Mammies came to be.

Who told you that?

Irish mythology is both a blessing and a curse for Irish women. On the one hand, it depicts a plethora of very powerful and influential women at the upper echelons of classical Irish society. On the other hand, as most Irish mythology was first transcribed by monks, strong women were treated with suspicion and aspersions were cast on their character.

Queen Meabh of Connacht is a good example of this. She is depicted in the *Táin Bó Cuailgne* as an ambitious and vain harridan who would sacrifice armies for the sake of her pride. But there is little about the other side of Meabh — no mention of her appearance in the smaller epic *Cuardach na Circe*

Doinne, Áille, Bige ('The Search for the Lovely Little Brown Hen'), where Meabh notices that one of her best layers is missing and eventually finds her under a hedge.

Much is made of Cuchulainn killing the savage hound of Culann with a hurley and sliotar – *not a word* about the countless times Meabh brought the under-age lads to training or washed the jerseys.

The gender imbalance in much of Irish folklore is further seen in the Fianna Cycle. In the tales of the Fianna, women are generally portrayed as scheming minxes with voracious and quixotic sexual appetites. On the other hand, the Fianna were lauded for hunting, jumping over branches at forehead height or pulling thorns from their feet. Life for them was like a particularly long and destructive stag-party, often with actual stags. Little is mentioned of the women of heroic Ireland who ran the villages and households, creating enough wealth for it to be sported away.

This historical travesty taught Mammy that most people are all talk, but someone still has to do the work.

That oul foreign yoke

Like the mythology, the stories of Ireland's struggles against our nearest neighbour's 'visit' are similarly imbalanced. The focus is more often on battles, Spanish and French armies arriving in the wrong place in the wrong year or spies sneaking away to tell the English what time things were kicking off at. Mammy must have been there in the background, but her views are not recorded, which is a pity. What, for example, did Aoife MacMurrough's mother think of her daughter's marriage to Strongbow?

And so in the narrative of the nation, Mammy does not feature. But that does not mean the years of English rule have not had a profound effect on her in two ways.

1. The failure of countless rebellions taught the Irish Mammy not to expect too much from life, particularly when men were doing the organizing.

2. Visitors are all very well until they outstay their welcome.

Prior to the twentieth century, the Irish Mammy is not recorded as having taken part in much direct action against the English — apart from one celebrated case.

In January 1651, Cromwell's army was poised to take Bagenalstown in County Carlow. The army encircled the town and sent messages to the townsfolk to surrender. Given the experience of previous towns at the hands of Cromwell's soldiers, the situation looked bleak. The story is told that the soldiers were surprised by a lone woman striding forcefully to the encampment and delivering a dressing-down to their general — a Lord Earl Wrottesly DeVere Horchester — telling him she was very disappointed in his behaviour, that he was impressing no one, and not only was he letting everyone else down but he was letting himself down as well. The upbraided general was said to have felt such inexplicable guilt that he suspended the siege and marched away. The incident is commemorated in the ballad 'The Passive Aggression of Bagenalstown'.

The most famous Mammy of Irish Nationalism is Countess Markievicz, who defended the Royal College of Surgeons and wounded a British sniper, but there were other Mammies: Therese Foley, who braved shellfire to bring a cough bottle to rebels in Boland's Mills; and Rita Duggan, who held up an entire British gunship because those on board were making too much noise at this hour.

The Irish language

Although not spoken by the majority of Irish Mammies, the Irish language still contains strong clues about her personality and outlook. An Ghaeilge is a most beautiful and expressive language. Its flowing and versatile sounds have been employed to produce love poetry and descriptions of nature – but its phlegmatic consonants are also ideal for no-nonsense dismissals of messers and wasters.

It is the Irish *seanfhocail* – wise old sayings – that best encapsulate the wisdom of Irish Mammies and serve as reminders that we could have done with some more of that wisdom in recent years. The main point of most *seanfhocail* is that happiness is fleeting and there's surely some misfortune around the corner (a bit like the end of an episode of *EastEnders*). They are best exemplified by the saying *'Bíonn gach duine go deas go dtéann bó ina gharraí'* (which directly translates as 'Everyone is nice until a cow gets in their garden' or 'It's all fun and games until someone loses an iris.')

Translates as 'Breeding breaks out through the eyes of a cat' or 'The father was the very same.'

Whatever her origins, history or influences, the Irish Mammy is very much a figure of the present – and now we need her more than ever.

2

There's No Place Like It

Where is the comrade of that sock, I wonder?

Definite articles

Some Irish Mammies work exclusively in the home; some don't. Regardless, for the smooth running of the house, all who live and originate there need to know that, like all states, it needs order. And for order, you need rules. *Bunreacht an Tí* – The Constitution of the House – guarantees these rules are adhered to. Without it, there is chaos.

ARTICLE I: **While you're under this roof …**

The Constitution is a guideline, but the final arbiter in all matters is Mammy. Her jurisdiction in this role can comprise, but not exclusively so, the following areas:

1.1 In the matter of whose turn it is to have the bath, please note: no right to a bath has been enshrined in the Constitution, and all bathers have responsibilities in this matter, specifically in the question of usage. Though it may not be stated explicitly, it is understood she did not mean for you to take *all* the hot water.

1.2 Who among a pair of quarrelling children is perceived to be whining and who has a legitimate claim to another biscuit.

1.3 Citizens are also instructed not to mind what their father has said, he shouldn't have said that at all without consulting Mammy and, furthermore: we'll see.

Where a situation occurs which has not been explicitly mentioned in the main provisos of Article I, Mammy may also instigate any proceedings whose justification is based entirely on the Memorandum of Understanding appended to this document; commonly known as the 'Because I said so' clause.

ARTICLE 3: **Make sure you put it back where you got it now.**

Citizens of the household have the right to make use of all handy things, provided such objects which by common consent are agreed to have a Safe Place shall be returned to that Safe Place once the period of usage has reasonably expired. The list of handy things comprises, but not exclusively, scissors, the Sellotape, the remote control, the charger for the mobile, the yoke for straining the tea and your father's Nice Pen.

ARTICLE 7: **I hope you didn't use the good scissors for that.**

The house provides for the scissorial needs of all its occupants, but this is contingent on 'fair usage' of aforementioned scissors. Fair usage means using the bad scissors for cutting paper and sausages; the good scissors are to be reserved primarily for cloth and hair. The sewing scissors are to be accorded similar respect and may attract even greater sanction if misused. Certain allowances will be made if the bad scissors can be demonstrably shown to have gone missing, but it is expected that a reasonable effort is subsequently made to locate the bad scissors — particularly as their absence may be due to a contravention of Article 3.

ARTICLE 8: **Are you still in the sitting room? … You're not. Well, if you wouldn't mind turning off the lights. We're trying to keep the bill down.**

The electricity is an essential utility for occupants; however it must be exploited sensibly. Where it is patently clear that there is no need at all for all these lights, the lights are to be turned off. Provided it does not contravene Article 24: *You'll ruin your eyesight reading in this bad light.*

ARTICLE 23: **Hold on to that, it might be useful for something.**

It is acknowledged that within the house not all objects will have a usefulness that is obvious to all residents and guests. But that is *no* reason to throw them out. That was the piece of string for your father's glasses. Mammy has her system and wishes you wouldn't go moving things.

ARTICLE 27: **There's no point in leaving that here, sure we won't eat it.**

It is the right of every Mammy and Himself to broaden their palate at precisely their own pace. Mammy undertakes to treat with civility the introduction of oul spicy foods at inopportune moments; however, she reserves the right to place those foods in the press, where they will gradually work their way to the back until found a number of years later. To avoid such an eventuality, visitors should ideally not bring that stuff at all. For reference, it is advisable to read the guidelines in the Addendum, with particular reference to the section entitled 'Tinned Fruit Cocktail – An eighty-year journey to universal acceptance'.

ARTICLE 30: That's the good tea towel. Hold on a second and I'll get you a rag.

The house supports fully the aspiration of all occupants to tidy up after themselves. However, where this conflicts with the established Hierarchy of Cleaning Cloths – commonly known as the Tea Towel Iceberg – this shall take precedence, and it is the duty of all occupants to spare the good tea towel or at least ask before you go using it on the floor. Adherence to Article 30 of *Bunreacht an Tí* means having a strong knowledge of the Tea Towel Iceberg.

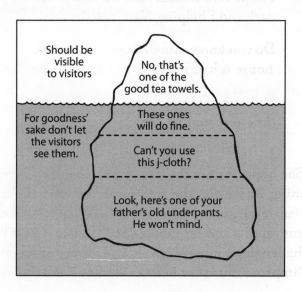

Saint Anthony

Humans being human, the rules of the house will at some stage be broken. Things will not be put back where they were found. Things will get lost. When Irish Mammy loses something, her mind flips through the possible scenarios:

- I must have put it down when the phone rang.

- It might have slipped out when I was hoovering.

- I hope now it didn't fall out in the car park and I helping Nan into the car.

- Do you know something? I swear this house is haunted.

- Did one of the children move it when they were home?

She hopes it's not the last option. Adult children coming home for the weekend, full of pent-up get-up-and-go energy after a week spent writing status reports and creating value for their clients in a challenging business environment, are desperate to 'improve' things at home. '*Mammy, wouldn't you be better off putting all of them on the one shelf?'* They want to put things in a more logical order, but all they've done is moved a crucial object (whose significance they haven't spotted) away from a Safe Place. Adult child will get a phone call.

'You didn't come across an envelope when you were tidying the cupboard, did you?'

'No, I didn't see any envelope.' (Lie; adult child vaguely remembers an envelope with something written on it, and it *may* have been thrown out.)

'Ah, you must have. I had all the tablets for your father written on it.'

'But why didn't you put it in a Safe Place?'

'It *was* in a Safe Place. I wish you'd ask me before moving things. I know where everything goes, you see. I'll have to say a prayer to Saint Anthony now.'

Christian hagiography attests to the existence of a number of Saint Anthonys, so she needs to pick the right one. St Anthony of Antioch lived in the Egyptian desert. Over the course of his life, despite being beaten by the devil and tempted with luxuries by the villagers, St Anthony of Antioch sought deeper and deeper austerity. It's not him she wants. He is the patron saint of the ECB (European Central Bank). The Saint Anthony who finds the backs of earrings stuck in Irish Mammies' jumpers is Saint Anthony of Padua. He is also known as Saint Anthony of Lisbon — presumably because, like the referendum, sometimes you have to ask him the same question twice.

He is also the patron saint of elderly people, but that may just be because he is always around at their houses looking for their glasses case.

St Anthony is said to have got his powers because he lost a book of psalms at his monastery. Another monk had accidentally taken it away, and Saint Anthony miraculously recovered it.

Irish Mammy calls on St Anthony of Padua, and he gets to work, negotiating with ghosts, guilt-tripping adult children and searching Safe Places until the object is found. He has to. Egyptian deserts and hell hath no fury like a frustrated Irish Mammy.

He's not the only saint employed by Mammy.

Name . . . . St Therese
From . . . . Lisieux
Famous for . . . The s. . .
            sou. . .
Novenability . . Ver. . .
            High

Name . . . . Padre Pio
From . . . . Italy
Famous for . . . Stigmata

Novenability . . . . . . High

. . e . . . . Anthony
. . . . Padua
. . us for . . . Finding
            things
. . ability . . Low

Visitors

The rules don't just apply internally. Visitors, too, have obligations. They need to understand the impact of their arrival.

It starts at the door.

Who's this at the door?

Mammy is busy, so if you are going to interrupt her make sure you have a good reason. The following pointers should ensure you get a fair hearing:

If you are collecting for something — be young.

Never make assumptions.

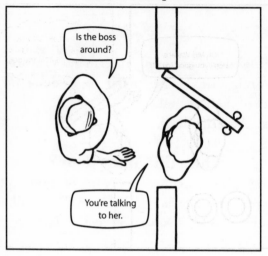

Leave both hands free for grabbing a dog's paws, especially if you are wearing a nice coat.

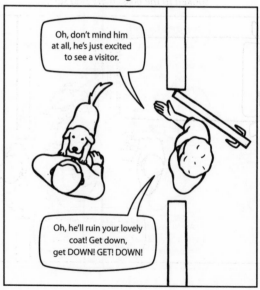

You never saw this.

It doesn't matter who you've made the deal with. If you haven't spoken to the boss, there's no sale.

Visitors don'ts

For the non-commercial visitor, it is imperative that they don't:

- Mind the mess. In fact, say 'What mess? Oh, for goodness' sake, Mrs Fitzgerald, you should see our place.' You won't convince her, but she'll appreciate the gesture.

- Arrive early.

- Arrive on time.

- Arrive less than ten minutes late.

- Call during *Coronation Street*.

- Refuse normal tea. Just drink it and keep your mouth shut about it. The merest mention of a tea that is not *tea* tea will spark an ill-advised purchase of some jasmine-rose-petal-gingko concoction that you will be forced to drink every time you return, because you are known as the person who drinks the 'quare tea'.

- 'Drop in' unannounced.

The last don't is the most important. If you call in unannounced, the Irish Mammy will spend the entire visit lamenting the poor quality of the welcome: 'I'm sorry now I haven't any more to offer ye. If ye'd have only rung to say ye were coming.'

It is likely that the Irish Mammy would say this even if she just happened to have an entire roasted pig left over from the previous day and the table groaned beneath the weight of sweetbreads, game, venison and succulent mysterious fruits from the Levant. The point is, you committed a cardinal error — you caught Irish Mammy on the hop. She'll cover up any distress but, rest assured, while she's out scalding the teapot, she's screaming silently into her fist.

Diary of Irish Mammy's cat

The house can also be home to pets — the most inscrutable of whom is Pussy.

MONDAY

Sometimes I think she doesn't understand me at all. I simply want to walk around for a bit to weigh up my options. Is that so wrong?

TUESDAY

Today was nearly the best day ever, until somebody stuck their oar in …

WEDNESDAY

Don't get me started … What's the point in having a favourite chair if every Tom, Dick and Harry gets to sit on it? I wouldn't mind but she doesn't even like Mona.

THURSDAY

I cannot believe how I'm being treated here — especially in my condition. I've a good mind to ring Joe Duffy about it.

Drying

'We have a tumble dryer all right, but we use it sparingly. It's very heavy on current.'

The Atlantic doesn't just bring colds and sniffles — it brings another challenge to the authority of the Irish Mammy: drying clothes — a laborious task anywhere in the world, but a particular chore in Ireland due to the DAMP (Drifting Atlantic Moisture Precipitate).

Our proximity to the cold liquid in the Atlantic causes condensation to form on the country in much the same way that droplets appear on a pint glass.

This is complicated by the fact that Ireland was built on a flood plain without planning permission. There was never supposed to be a country here.

As if that wasn't bad enough, building regulations were flouted and Ireland is the only country in the world without a damp-proof course. The diagram below shows the difference between Ireland and Spain in cross-section.

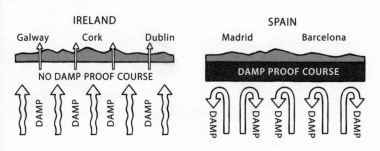

The War on Damp shouldn't just be Mammy's problem. Hasn't she raised a family of fostúchs well able to put clothes drying themselves? Himself sometimes does give a hand but it is still Irish Mammy who knows best the difference between damp and aired.

The central battleground is the hot press. As we saw earlier, the hot press has been an emblem of humanity for thousands of years. Its cultural significance is clearly visible in some of the most iconic works of art. Art historians speculate that Michelangelo may be making reference to the hot press in his work on the wall of the Sistine Chapel.

This is best seen if we place the two side by side. Almost certainly, Michelangelo regarded the Last Judgement as a giant celestial hot press.

You can see that the central focus of the painting is in the shape of a hot water cylinder. Look closely and you will notice how the fate of humanity echoes the 'salvation' of clothes in the press. In the upper reaches of the press are the good linen, the pillow cases, the blouses. Like angels, their future is dry and secure.

On the sides of the painting and the hot press are the souls and T-shirts awaiting their judgement, hoping that they will be dried and not found wanting.

Then, at the bottom are the damned — the murderers, thieves, heretics and odd socks that fell behind the cylinder and will never be recovered.

There are no plenary indulgences in the hot press — no short cuts. Each item must serve its time in the hope of salvation.

> 'Where did you get that jumper from? ...
> Which side of the hot press? ... That's still
> *damp*. Anything on that side is *still damp*.'

Occasionally — so rarely that it is the first or second item on the News when it happens — there will be that Day of Days — when there's good drying out.

Everything will go in the washing machine — curtains and net curtains, duvets and duvet covers, pillows and pillow cases. And on that day ...

> 'I went out to the line — I'd say it was only an
> hour later — and I felt the clothes and they
> were *bone dry*. 'magine!'

With drying like this, Irish Mammy looks wistfully in the house at the other things that could do with being put out – carpets, beds, mattresses, children. Then she waits, *Crouching Tiger, Hidden Dragon*-like, ready to move the instant she feels the first spatters of rain.

For the objects that are not easily hot-pressed or put out on the line, the second strategy in the fight against the Axis of Damp is put into place: airing.

> 'You could get an awful cold from a bed that wasn't aired properly.'

Irish Mammy has a store of anecdotes to serve as dire warning against the evils of an unaired bed. Such is the importance of an aired bed, visitors who intend to stay overnight but haven't given prior warning may be turned away. Better that you slept on the road than on a damp sheet.

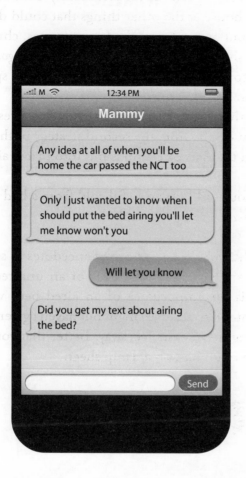

Weather

Over the years, nothing has had a more profound effect on the Irish Mammy than the Irish weather. The only thing she can trust about it is that it can't be trusted. For each situation, she has a perfect phrase to sum up the national mood. Whatever her origins, history or influences, the Irish Mammy is very much a figure of the present — and now we need her more than ever.

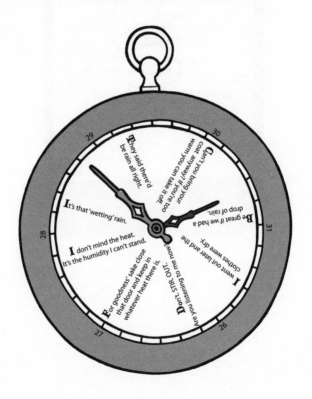

They said there'd be rain all right.

Can't you bring your warm anyway? If you're too warm you can take it off.

It's that 'wetting' rain.

Be great if we had a drop of rain.

I don't mind the heat. It's the humidity I can't stand.

I went out later and the clothes were dry.

For goodness' sake close that door and keep in whatever heat there is.

Don't. STIR. OUT. Are you listening to me now?

3

Mind Yourself

Off up to bed with you now. That's the only
thing for it.

Health and well-being are fertile grounds for conversation. Neighbours, husbands/partners, children — they all have enough wrong with them to keep the chat going.

Top five health-related things to say

- I saw him all right and he was very shook.

- I *knew* I hadn't seen her at Mass in a while.

- Where did you get that cough, I wonder.

- A quadruple bypass — 'magine.

- You may be sure we got our jabs. We're not taking any chances.

Of course, when the talking's over, the ailments have to be treated.

There's one going

There is nothing better in the human experience than a child's path through life as they explore the world around them. Their physical and mental selves develop, they embrace new challenges, they create their own tiny corner of history. Irish Mammy's job is to ensure they don't get a cough or a cold while doing so. While distracted by their voyage of discovery, children can't be trusted to look after themselves properly.

So Irish Mammy needs to keep them under surveillance. Ireland's location makes this a constant job – and Science is not on Mammy's side.

In geographical terms, Ireland is an island with a temperate climate that is heavily influenced by the North Atlantic drift and a prevailing wind from the south-west.

In more practical terms, Ireland is sitting in an awful draught.

There are two main ways in which colds are contracted. The draughts are the most pernicious, chiefly because this is the reason most Irish Mammies themselves catch a cold. The draught occurs most often while they are at a gathering or a group occasion where they have no choice about where they are sitting. There is the dark suspicion that Mammy's anti-cold measures have been breached by the perfidy of a male.

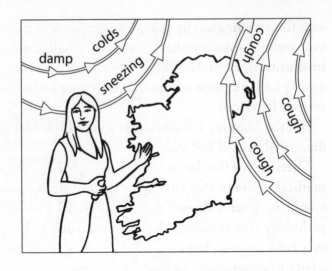

'One of the young Costigans — I'd say it was Barry — must have left the door open, and I got an awful cold sitting in a draught below at the school.'

The second type of cold-transmission is inexcusable: Self-inflicted Due to a Lack of Sense. It is the cold contracted by a child aged between zero and forty-two years of age.

It is inexcusable, because the child may have done that which they were expressly warned against — discarding a coat too early in the year or sitting on a damp step.

Children hate coats. They get in the way, making essential childish activities difficult. Show a child a muddy area which contains wheel-ruts and puddles — and therefore the possibility to hack out a canal with their wellington by using it to drain water from one puddle into another — and they will almost involuntarily begin to remove their coat. Similarly, when playing a game of chase, the flailing hood is a serious handicap.

But the Mammy knows that as soon as the coat is discarded, a cold will start.

Then there's the damp step. Although there is no medical evidence that sitting on a damp step causes a cold in your kidneys, nor any official medical pathology that indicates there is even such a thing as a cold in your kidneys, it's hard to gainsay the advice of generations of Irish Mammies.

The damp step has even made it into TV courtroom drama, as this excerpt from a *Matlock* script shows.

SCENE: COURTROOM.

The case is reaching its climax. Lawyer Ben Matlock is cross-examining his final witness.

Matlock:
Now can you tell me again what you were doing on the afternoon of the murder?

Witness:
On Wednesday afternoon I was going to the drugstore as I usually do, when I saw Mrs O'Sullivan sitting on her doorstep.

Matlock:

Let me stop you right there, Ms Lafontaine. Now you are saying that my client, Mrs O'Sullivan, an Irish Mammy, was sitting on a step?

Witness:

That's right, Mr Matlock.

Matlock:

What was the weather like on Wednesday – can you remember?

Witness:

Well, of course it rained in the morning, but then the afternoon was sunny.

Matlock:

So you are saying that my client, Irish Mammy, was sitting outside on a step that was still potentially damp and cold from the rain. Is that what you are saying?

Witness: (*blushes*)

I ... uh ... I guess so, Mr Matlock.

Matlock:

Isn't that just a little hard to believe?

Witness:

I ... I ... don't know. Look, Mr Matlock, I saw what I saw. She was there. She killed him! (*looks at judge*) I swear!

Matlock:

I don't think you saw my client there at all,
did you? She would not sit on a damp step.
You didn't see her, because she wasn't there.
It was you sitting on that step. After you
killed Franklyn Thomas.

Witness: (*crying*)

Everything was fine until *she* came along.
Always making him tea and sandwiches …
He never even noticed me after that. I …
I went around to his house with some
buns … I wanted to reason with him …
He laughed at me … Said he was grand for
buns … I got angry … Oh, Mr Matlock,
I loved him so much.

Matlock (*softly*):

So you killed him … No further questions,
your honour.

SCENE ENDS.

Regardless of where they came from, there's
far more than 'one going'. Colds, chills,
sniffles (not to mention the odd bout of
double pneumonia), and Irish Mammies will
be joined in battle until the end of time – or
at least until the weather clears up a bit anyway.

Do bottle it up

Of all the ailments to arrive back at the ancestral home with, a cough is the severest indictment of a mother's main suspicion: her child is not looking after him or herself properly. As a matter of fact, unless he or she married Doctor Spock, nothing would reassure an Irish mother that her child would get the same level of fussing in the big bad world as they got at home.

If getting a cough is unfortunate, not treating it is foolishness.

> 'Do you have a cough bottle?'

> 'Erm, not yet, haven't got around to getting one.'

> 'No cough bottle?!!!'

The look and tone of horror is the same as if one had declared one's interest in becoming a Scientologist.

Where an Irish Mammy has any kind of power at all in a house, that house will have a cough bottle, a sticky brown container occupying the same place in the cupboard, for years.

It's one of those memories of childhood that are

literally a blur. You cough yourself awake and then, gently materializing in the glare of a Solus 75W bulb, is Mammy, armed with a small white plastic spoon brimming with pink liquid. Sometimes, on the nights where you were still a little sleepy, the handover of the floating spoon from mother to mouth went slightly awry and some drops fell on to your pyjama collar, where it made for a sweet snack before falling back to sleep.

At some stage later in the night, like one of those ads which (completely scientifically) show some sort of 'rapid' or 'fast-acting relief' spreading down the gullet, the cough bottle would go to work. A cough which previously sounded like a seal barking to warn the herd of an approaching orca was transformed into a much softer, phlegmatic, shrapnelly affair:

Cough? Cough? Couuuugh-bleuuhgh! Bleuuhgh! Blahaghhhgagle.

Of course, as everyone knows, what was actually happening was that 'the pseudoephedrine is triggering a release of endogenous norepinephrine from storage vesicles in presynaptic neurons', but that's a little difficult to represent in a five-second video on the telly.

It takes a while for adult children living away from home to take the same care of themselves. Without proper mothering, you will leave a tickly cough untreated until it becomes a big cough. You're kidding yourself, because you can't hide a cough from Mammy. Even in a phone-call.

'How is that cough of yours now?'

'It's fine, it's just a ti—<cough>—ickle, I'll soldier <cough> <cough> on<cough> <Cough> <Cough> <**COUGH**> <COUGH><COUGH> <Honngh> <HONNGH> <**HONNGH**>.'

The cough is out of the bag. The seal imper-sonation has done the damage.

'Get down to the chemist straight away and get a cough bottle. Do you hear me now?'

The chemist stocks some 'natural-based' remedies, but you know Mammy is waiting for a cough-bottle report and she won't brook any of that organic nonsense. She won't be happy until you get a cough bottle made by a multinational, preferably one that is a major contributor to the US Republican party. In a few years the ingredients will probably be the subject of an investigative documentary, but for now they are all safely wrapped up in 'a demulcent syrup to aid a restful sleep'.

After spending a couple of nights demulced off your head, it should be safe enough to risk phoning home to put it to the test.

> 'Oh it's much better. Listen: <cough?> <cough?> <cough?>...< no cough>. See? All better. '

> 'That's great. Didn't I tell you the cough bottle is your only man?'

Top reminiscible diseases and 'health events'

- Will I ever forget that winter? All three of ye had **croup**. Can you imagine that? Three small girls under the age of five. And what's more, your father in bed with a cold.

- Do you remember when you had **whooping cough**? I was up and down that stairs with the kettle.

- We were all set to go. Next thing the phone rings. It's the school. 'We think Deirdre has **chickenpox**,' they said. And that was the end of Malaga.

- I can't get over how much sleep you need now, when you **wouldn't sleep** for me until you were about *two*.

- I don't know what you were doing but didn't you **swallow the crayon**. And Dr Phelan was as *cool* about it. 'Don't be worrying,' says he. 'That'll pass naturally.'

Text on book:

MAMMIES' GUINNESS BOOK OF TEMPERATURES

①

104! When you had mumps, you poor little mite

4

Lessons Learned

They're learning nothing below in that school.

Irish Mammies have helped generations of kids through the school years. iPads have replaced the duster across the back of the head as educational tools. The balance of power has changed from 'Well, if you got a slap you must have been bold,' to 'My client has instructed me...' Despite all this, the end result is still very familiar: the Leaving Cert and with it, the annual chatter about POINTS.

> ... Oh, it's all go here. Áine says Saoirse is happy with the results – 480 she got. I'm told that's good... Yes, she should be fine for the course... Business and Something in Dublin... Ah, you're very good... All the prayers came in handy I'd say... Yes, they were very worried about the English... Some poet didn't come up... I'd never seen her mother as STRESSED about it... Look Áine, I said, even if she doesn't get the points I'm sure it'll be fine. NO, MAMMY, says she. It WON'T be fine. Saoirse'll have to repeat... Well, I stayed out of it after that.

All the education in the world won't teach you sense. The Leaving Cert syllabus could do with a bit of input from Irish Youth's first and greatest educator. Here's how the exam papers might look if Irish Mammies set the questions.

Coimisiún na Scruduithe Stáit
State Examinations Commission

LEAVING CERTIFICATE EXAMINATIONS

MATHS AH YOU'LL DO THE HONOURS
FRIDAY 6TH JUNE – AFTERNOON 2.00 to 4.30

SECTION A – HARD SUMS

1. **(i) Derive Newton's Law of Cooling using a calculus differential equation.**

    (ii) In the name of God, how is that tea gone cold if it was only made five minutes ago?

    Note: Extra marks will be awarded if you can prove that teapot mustn't have been scalded at all.

2. **Using the Irish Mammy's Law of Worry:**

    $$W = \frac{C_{sw}}{S}$$

    Where:
    W = Level of Worry

    C_{sw} = Constant Source of Worry

    S = Sense

    Answer me this: What am I to do with you at all?

Coimisiún na Scruduithe Stáit
State Examinations Commission

LEAVING CERTIFICATE EXAMINATIONS

GEOGRAPHY DON'T EVEN THINK OF DOING PASS
FRIDAY 6TH JUNE – MORNING 9.30 to 12.00

SECTION A – EXCUSE ME NOW

1. **What do you mean 'Out'? Out where?**

   (i) Nowhere

   (ii) Just out

   (iii) At a friend's

SECTION B – PARISH NEWS

2. **With reference to the supplied aerial photograph, would you have any idea:**

   (i) Who's building that big house over near Hartigans?

   (ii) Where did they get the money for it at all?

   (If you refer to an inheritance in your answer, <u>please</u> specify WHICH aunt)

   (iii) Is it a married couple that's in there or is it one of these 'modern' arrangements?

Coimisiún na Scruduithe Stáit
State Examinations Commission

LEAVING CERTIFICATE EXAMINATIONS

PASS HISTORY? HAVE A BIT OF SENSE
WEDNESDAY 11TH JUNE – AFTERNOON 2.00 to 4.50

SECTION A – HANDY ENOUGH ONES

1. **What were you like at all, as a small child?**

    (i) Fierce lively

    (ii) A holy terror

    (iii) A divil altogether

    (iv) Oh stop!

2. **'Twas far away from *what*, you were reared?**

    (i) iPads

    (ii) Hummus

    (iii) *The Voice*

    (iv) It

Coimisiún na Scruduithe Stáit
State Examinations Commission

LEAVING CERTIFICATE EXAMINATIONS

BIOLOGY I BET TOM MURPHY'S DOING HONOURS
TUESDAY 10TH JUNE – AFTERNOON 2.00 to 5.00

SECTION A – MINDING YOURSELF

1. How did you get that cold?

(i) Went out without your coat

(ii) Sat in a draught

(iii) Sat on that damp step after I told you not to

Refer to the attached diagrams in your answer.

(i)

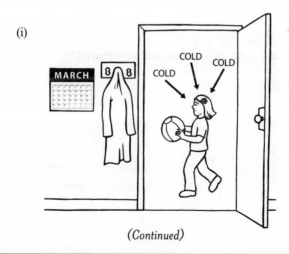

(*Continued*)

61

(ii)

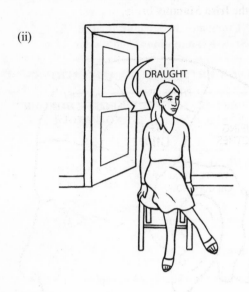

(iii)

2. With reference to the diagram, discuss the functions of the main lobes of the Irish Mammy brain.

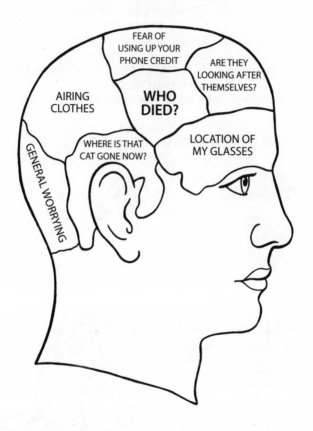

Coimisiún na Scruduithe Stáit
State Examinations Commission

LEAVING CERTIFICATE EXAMINATIONS

CHEMISTRY LOOK WE'LL GET YOU GRINDS OR SOMETHING
TUESDAY 17TH JUNE – AFTERNOON 2.00 to 5.00

SECTION A – EXPERIMENTING, I SUPPOSE

1.

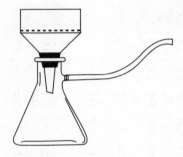

Is this yours? It's not what I think it is, is it? I hope you're not mixed up in anything now.

(Continued)

SECTION B – IN YOUR ELEMENT

1. With reference to the attached periodic table, outline the chief characteristics of each group with reference to the Irish Mammy's Principles of Danger.

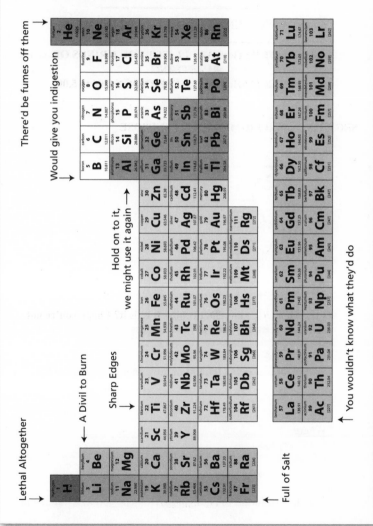

There'd be fumes off them

Would give you indigestion

Hold on to it, we might use it again

Lethal Altogether

A Divil to Burn

Sharp Edges

Full of Salt

You wouldn't know what they'd do

Coimisiún na Scruduithe Stáit
State Examinations Commission

LEAVING CERTIFICATE EXAMINATIONS

PHYSICS I KNOW YOU WON'T NEED HONOURS FOR ARTS BUT STILL …
MONDAY 16TH JUNE – MORNING 9.30 to 12.00

SECTION A – THE CURRENT

1.

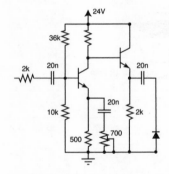

I'd say this is very hard on electricity, is it?

2. With reference to the Irish Mammy's Theory of Relative-ity:

$E = mc^2$

Where:
E = Everyone
m = might be
c^2 = your second cousin

wouldn't you want to be fierce careful who you were talking to?

5

The Messages

They're gone very dear in there altogether.

The weekly shop

She's making a list; she's checking it twice. She's going to find out who's home for the weekend and whether she needs an extra sliced pan or not. Irish Mammy is preparing for the weekly shop. Now she just has to find her bags-for-life and she is ready to go.

It is estimated that since the Irish government imposed a levy on plastic bags, approximately four million cubic feet of space has been freed up in the presses of Irish Mammies. Mammy always stored plastic bags, tucked inside one another, in anticipation of some unspecified Armageddon. Once the tax was introduced, in the absence of regular infusions of new bags, the EU-intervention-sized plastic mountain was gradually diminished. Now, in most homes, only a battle-hardened group of bags-for-life remain. The assortment of Lidl, Tesco, SuperValu and Dunnes bags forms a motley crew of mercenaries, their colours frayed from the batterings of a thousand scrunchings, some among them containing flakes of onion skin, a receipt and a long-forgotten packet of stock cubes.

Once at the shops, Mammy faces obstacles that are perfectly surmountable but annoying nonetheless.

Sliced pan - a good few

get prescriptions renewed

fruit cocktail
a roast
spread
rashers & sausages
flour
baking soda
Daz
cranberry juice
bananas

cotton wool
plasters
Multi vitamins
Sudocrem
Sonjela — The paper
matches
plain biscuits
custard creams

Silvikrin
Mass card for
Mrs O'

POSTAS
0055
IS30686
éire

69

'Why do they *keep* moving everything around? Aren't they very cute now?'

At the checkouts, Mammy flinches as she sees someone packing bags for charity. Yes, of course, the smiling children in outsized T-shirts are a credit to their parents and their school, but Mammy would much rather pack the bags herself.

'Where had they put the sliced ham? Only in with the raw chicken. Of course I said nothing — just gave them the few bob.'

At least they're human.

Suits you down to the ground

Once in adulthood, shopping trips between Irish Mammies and daughters are collaborative, collegial affairs. Mammy and daughter exchange tips. They confide. Mammy's 'finding it hard to get something for Una's wedding'. Her daughter promises they'll 'go for a spin to a boutique'.

On the other hand, Mammy regards her son as very much a work in progress. For adult sons, there is only one shopping trip left to make:

> 'We'll have to get you a suit now, for your interviews.'

Now, under normal circumstances, any self-respecting 22-year-old male should be capable of buying a suit for himself, but this is the suit for the interviews. It needs to give an impression of solid dependability as the candidate tries to convince the recruiter that working as a sun-lounge attendant in Nantucket last summer was bona fide experience of 'working in a dynamic and fast-paced environment and instigating a number of value-creation initiatives'.

Nothing can be left to chance with this suit. Mammy needs to manage this one. As she says herself: 'Wisha you wouldn't know what he'd arrive in with.'

It is likely that a son will have more control over his Holy Communion outfit than over his graduation or interview suit. As a seven-year-old boy, his views on appropriate attire were much closer to his mother's than now. In the meantime, he has developed opinions.

The colour of the suit will lie somewhere in a very narrow spectrum — somewhere in between navy and mid-grey. Any requests or choices initiated by the son himself are indulged up to a point. There is an approximately 10-minute window where he can literally suit himself. The window is then shut gently but firmly.

He may have arrived to the draper's with vaguely idealistic notions about what a suit should feel like — perhaps a slightly crumpled linen affair redolent of the man from Del Monte, or a gentlemanly tweed ensemble with high waistband after he saw a Cary Grant film.

He admires himself in the mirror, feeling his 'personality' is being finally expressed in suit form. 'Well, what do ye think?'

Cary Grant never dealt with an Irish Mammy. Irish Mammy coordinates raised eyebrows with the draper before selecting a sensible suit that she had her eye on all the time. Like two Jeeveses they collaborate on persuading Mr Wooster back to the appropriate course of action.

The choice of draper is crucial here. The right draper is about five feet eight inches tall. He has neat, greying hair, the sort of hair that was greying ever since his wedding photograph was taken and will remain at this level of grey for another 50 years. Not a hair on his head is out of place. He moves in his own suit as if it were a second three-piece skin. His eyes are calm. He doesn't need the sale — another will be along soon.

The sensible suit is tried on.

'Oh that's much better,' says Mammy. 'You don't want to be drawing too much attention to yourself.'

'Listen to your mother — she's right, you know. For an interview, the suit should be in the background. Plenty of time for "fashion" when you've got the job.'

He almost spits out the word 'fashion'. The son doesn't even notice how incongruous it is for a man selling clothing to disdain the word 'fashion'. He is defeated.

'Now do you hear that? I think it looks lovely on you. Makes you look very handsome.'

The young man smiles weakly. His dreams of being a town gent, a Carnaby Street swell, for the time being at least, put back on the peg.

Fear to thread

And what about these blue ones?
Look! The elasticated waistband.
He looks at the trousers
She's holding in her hand.
His protests are reasoned,
She has to understand
These slacks will see him outcast,
A pariah in the land.
But she bats aside his 'whinges',
His gripes are swiftly panned.
Aren't you fierce fashion-conscious
For a small boy? They're grand.

6

Enough Excitement

When would I find the time to sit down?

Nothing in them oul newspapers

It's Sunday, mid-morning. With a dramatic *fffffhlump!* the newspapers are deposited in living rooms across the country. Different papers figure in every family's pile, but where there is an Irish Mammy in the house, there is a good chance that somewhere in that pile will be the *Sunday Independent*.

The familiar masthead sprawls on coffee tables and the sides of armchairs up and down the country. Long after the news goes stale, it is still to be found lining shelves and cutlery drawers.

Irish Mammies and Himselves know where they stand with it. They won't like all of the articles. Indeed, there will be many exasperated harrumphs at the general carry-on in it as the reporter 'gets up close and personal' with someone who used to be a singer of some sort but now 'works in the media-consultancy business'.

Some of it will go unread and be seen next nestling behind the coal bucket. The fresh young face of some young slip of a thing writing about the perils of dating and 'the emotional jungle out there' will wrinkle into flames, their pearls of wisdom never discovered, as the kindling takes hold.

But there is enough news and views in *Th'Independent* to keep Mammies buying it week after week. Often it makes the news as well as breaking it. It is as ingrained in the routine of Sunday morning as Mass was/still is for some, and no matter what the imperfections, if there's one thing an Irish Mammy values, it's routine.

The most weighty paper is the *Sunday Times*, but rather like sweetcorn, much of its inner bulk may not be consumed. One piece is guaranteed to be dog-eared: The Culture. With its curmudgeonly TV and film reviews (Mammy takes a sneaky pleasure in seeing a new home-grown reality TV show being eviscerated in a few cranky sentences), it also has the easiest to use TV listings. The seven days of information are particularly useful in tracking the sometimes confusing deviations in the broadcast time of *Coronation Street*.

Also featuring quite frequently is the *Sunday World*, the front page often focusing on ALL THE CRIME EVERYWHERE! with headlines such as LOOK OUT! HE'S IN THE SHED! – thus confirming

Irish Mammy's suspicions of vast underground hangars in urban areas full of criminals ready to embark on a spree. She will then delicately tiptoe over the page containing 'Sexy Sabrina, 19, a student, who's 100% behind the Boys in Green', chuckling later as an intrepid reporter in a bikini splashes around in a pothole with a gamey farmer until she eventually alights on that dacent man – Brian D'Arcy.

'Wisha poor ould Brian D'Arcy never did anyone any harm and they're going after him. Haven't they better things to be doing now?'

For a small but loyal coterie of Mammies, the *Irish Catholic* is their only refuge from a barrage of bad news about the Church. They are not in denial but are glad of the chance to read about grand priests, find out news about prayer campaigns and to get a nice surprise when they find out that someone famous they thought was a fierce pagan has gone a bit Catholic in their old age.

'You wouldn't think it now to look at him, would you?'

Cuttings

To a lesser extent, local newspapers will feature. Their circulation in Irish Mammy households peaks when there is a possibility of a mention.

'You got a mention in the paper. I've cut it out and I'll send you a photocopy.'

'The Mention': There was a time when humans

rarely saw their name printed in any public arena apart from when they died – which was obviously too late – so getting a Mention in the paper had a certain cachet. It didn't matter if the Mention was only of the 'also in attendance were …' variety, although it was preferable if you did something more noteworthy and warranted a longer piece.

For the child who has got the Mention, the notoriety is thrilling, but fades fast. The child may forget the event which caused the Mention. But that is not the end of it. It has been preserved by Irish Mammy in a Cutting.

Long before Browsers, Bookmarks, Favourites, Digg, Pinterest, Reddit, spam links which say 'You really should watch this' (and then send a picture of a scantily clad female to everyone in your address book), there was the Cutting.

Though it is largely a thing of the past, there is nothing nicer than whiling away the afternoon riffling through a shoebox of cuttings. Sometimes the cuttings have not been cut at all and the whole page, or even the whole newspaper, has been retained, which can create its own problems.

You could stare at it for a while, thinking, 'She must have kept it for something,' and hoping that the real reason will jump out at you. Eventually the minor triumphs reveal themselves: Coming second in a table quiz organized by the Pioneers; being 'unused sub' for Éire Óg in a defeat for the under-16s at Fr Cogan Field; or being 'also in the chorus' at a Macra Variety 'do'.

Treasa Costello and Paul Walsh receiving their degrees above at The College the other day. Photo Tim Donegan

...s asking for you ...a bit of a cold ...e electric blanket

We had a great day at the graduation. The rain held off

J. G.

Here is a cutting from the paper. Would you believe the fella next to Treasa is one of the Welshes. They had four boys and he's the youngest. All of them doctors imagine. They're no joke those Welshes. I sent a mass card to Mrs Price, the poor thing. She was asking very hard after you.

81

Outside of the shoebox, these cuttings/mentions of Children Doing Well would have criss-crossed the Irish Sea, the Atlantic and the World, as supporting documentation, in envelopes that were a little bit too fat just to contain a letter and unlikely to contain money.

Though a good news story, graduations can be an invidious clipping to send, particularly if they besiege a family who for many valid reasons may not have had graduations or any interest in them.

'There's another letter from Auntie Nóirín with more clippings of *effing* graduations.'

Irish Mammy magazine

For all of this choice, though, there is still something missing. No one magazine reaches out to the Mammies of Ireland and fulfils all their consumer requirements. It's time for *Irish Mammy Magazine*.

IRISH MAMMY MAGAZINE

FASHION
You'll grow into it

**'WASN'T
'ROM OUR
;IDE THEY
;OT IT**

*he heartbreak
f 'oddness'*

**MARY
(ENNEDY**

n't she great!

**YOUR CHILD:
SENSIBLE,
FLIGHTY OR
A BITTEEN
WILD?**

*Take our fun new
questionnaire*

**EATING THINGS UP
N THE BEDROOM:**

e great electric blanket/hot water bottle debate

IS YOUR CHILD
Sensible, Flighty or a Bitteen Wild?

You need someone to bring you to a removal, and you ask your son or daughter – what happens?

A: He was a great help altogether – he left work early and everything and brought me over to it. Not a bit of grumbling out of him.

B: She was good to bring me and … I don't like to be saying anything but the Lord save us. I didn't think she knew Tom Deasy at all but she was crying non-stop all the way through. She was nearly crying more than Philomena. The Deasys were looking over, and what must they have been thinking. Says she, 'I'm just a very emotional person.'

C: He made a pure show of me. The removal was at seven. I waited for him. Five past seven, no sign. In the end I had to ring Peadar Casey to bring me. *Half eleven* this ludraman bowls up in a taxi. I'm still not talking to him.

It was Rag Week at your child's university – how did he or she mark the occasion?

A: I think they had some sort of a fancy-dress party all right. He went out of here dressed as a sailor – well, the top, anyway; he was still wearing his jeans. They had a good time socializing by all accounts.

B: Oh, don't be talking to me. She's after quitting the degree. Says she, 'Mam I felt "stifled".'

C: I'm still only hearing bits of the story. There was a gang of them drinking at half ten in the morning, and he must have got mixed up with a bad crowd because next thing Pauline Doran is on the phone saying there's a riot up the town, and says she Liam is after being taken away in a squad car. Someone said he was seen throwing a traffic cone in the window of the St Vincent de Paul shop.

Your child has appeared on a reality TV programme – which one was it?

A: Didn't *Celebrity Bainisteoir* come to Rosdowney? It was all go. Sean was a sub but he came on in the final. They lost but it was great for the area.

B: She went in for this *Dragon's Den* thing, selling these crystals for homeopathy or something. But she didn't get any call to go on it.

C: Now he told me he was doing it for a laugh, but he went on that oul *Tallafornia* – Oh, the Lord Save us, what he DIDN'T get up to on that show. I can't go outside the door.

What do you think of your son/daughter's choice of partner?

A: Well now, of course he's gay and he doesn't tell us a bit about anyone. I'm dying to meet any of his *partners*, but I won't say a word till he's good and ready.

B: The latest fella now is a drummer. He's been all over the world doing the African drumming, she tells me – although he lives at home with his mother now. Apparently, he says, 'The bottom has fallen out of the corporate market.'

C: 'Tis like *EastEnders* with him these days. They're breaking up and they're back together. I think myself he should have stuck with the last girl. This one has notions.

Do you still love him/her unconditionally?

A: Ah, he's a grand boy. He's very good to his mother to give him his due.

B: Oh shur of course – there's never a dull moment with that girl indeed.

C: Deedn' what else would I do? He has a good heart.

Did you answer:

Mostly A: A Rock of sense, that lad. Please God, now, he'll find someone nice.

Mostly B: Isn't she a scream? A bit flighty all right, but shur doesn't she keep it interesting?

Mostly C: Oh, haven't you your hands full? He's very wild all right, but he might grow out of it.

Turn it over to the other side so

For much of Irish modern history, there was a clear fault line running through society, and that fault line ran neatly between the TV channels RTÉ 1 and RTÉ 2.

On RTÉ 1 lived the safe programmes — *The Late Late Show*, *Winning Streak*, *the News*, *Prime Time*, *Would You Believe?*

On RTÉ 2 lived mainly the sport, the young people's programmes and also the edgy programmes that threatened the delicate balance within a household.

Opposite *The Late Late Show* lived the foreign films or, to use the collective term, 'quare films'. There was a time when watching a quare film was an undertaking fraught with risk.

When most people had only two channels but unfortunately only one TV, if you didn't want to see Peter Ustinov recount a hilarious anecdote, or old-school comedian Tom O'Connor telling a joke about Paddy, who appeared to have a fractious relationship with his mother-in-law, you were regarded as some sort of beardy type, or deviant, or both. Up and down the country, pretentious adolescents lobbied mothers every Friday to switch over to watch the foreign film.

But it was a delicate operation. Asking to change

channel from the Irish Mammy's option was like campaigning for democracy in a totalitarian state. Every subsequent bad thing to happen will be seen as an indictment not only of the incident itself but of the whole democratic process.

Therefore it was important to pretend noble motives for wanting to watch the foreign film, lest its content came back to bite you. 'But, Mammy, it's a very important Hungarian film, a cerebral commentary on the human condition.' Mostly she says no, but now and then when her annoyance spilled over at the umpteenth appearance of one of Gay's buddies in the *Late Late* studios, she relented.

It was the Greek philosopher Zeno who first posited the paradox that says that when you change channel, the probability of immediately seeing a graphic sex scene is directly proportional to the probability that you will be watching with your mother. Without fail, Frank Carson was replaced by a rapidly undressing foreign lady giving a rapidly undressing foreign man explicit instructions in subtitles as to what they both should do next. When the adolescent realized that the thing he hoped was going to happen was happening far too early – i.e. while his mother was still in the room – his mind would scream: 'Put your top back on, Magdalena, now is not the time!' But there was no stopping Magdalena as she proceeded to give Pavel a very important induction into the ways of Woman.

By contrast, the main channel was almost completely free of pitfalls — chiefly because it was full of people like us doing things that we liked, or at least could admit to liking. For a goodly proportion of Irish Mammies, that has not changed much in intervening years.

It's not enough to simply appear on RTÉ 1. To be truly loved by Irish Mammies, you need to pass the Giddy Test, or at the very least need to be considered a Great Oul Trooper.

Giddy
How not to be giddy

gid·dy /ˈgɪdi/ adjective

1. affected with vertigo; dizzy.

2. attended with or causing dizziness: a giddy climb.

3. frivolous and lighthearted; impulsive; flighty.

4. choosing ill-suited TV work rather hastily.

Everyone has to make a living, and sometimes perfectly nice public figures end up in situations where they incur the disapproval of Irish Mammies for their antics on TV. It is very easy to slip up. You could be a politician who has been gulled by the media into believing you are a great wit and then proceed to spend that wit, one half at a time, on a number of celebrity reality TV shows. You could be a healthy young adult who desperately wants to be famous and ends up cavorting with other desperadoes to avoid eviction on a sexually frank rural fly-on-the-wall show called *The Only Way is Easkey*. Or you are on *The Late Late Show* and so nervous you end up blurting out some bad language.

Redemption is possible and Mammy is willing to forgive if you try to emulate her heroes.

Fine and sensible

The following are felt to be sensible by Irish Mammies:

- Most newsreaders, except those appearing too much on 'giddy' programmes.

- Most weather forecasters, except those appearing too much on 'giddy' programmes.

- Pat Kenny, especially after he stopped doing *The Late Late Show*. 'I always thought it didn't suit him.'

- Miriam O'Callaghan, 'And she with *eight* children, 'magine.'

- Mary Kennedy – 'Ah, Mary is grand.'

Honourable mention for Great Oul Troopers

A subset of Fine and Sensible can also be regarded as Great Oul Troopers. These are media figures who have put in a long, seemingly undramatic shift of steady work. They don't 'shoot' to stardom. It's as though they've always been around. Examples of Great Oul Troopers include:

- Marty Morrissey – 'Jim Cashin was talking to him at a function, said he was all chat. No airs or anything like that.'

- Marty Whelan – 'And wasn't he right to let the hair go grey too?'

- Vincent Browne – 'How does he keep going at all? You wouldn't want to get on the wrong side of him I'd say … indeed no … haha.'

There's something about Marty

It's no coincidence that two great oul troopers are called Marty. If you've progressed from a Martin to a Marty, you've already signalled an openness, that you have a certain 'way about you'. It is the name of a man who is a master at exchanging harmless repartee with old ladies who have little clouds of white hair as they explain the significance of their little good-luck mascot for the show tonight. It is the name of a man who can ask an excitable Irish Mammy dressed in the county GAA windcheater who is in the process of rearing an entire full-back line of her own what she thinks the result of the match will be today. And it's the name of a man who will not be put off when the crowd behind her erupt in a *Yehoooo!* and tousles his distinctive hair.

There is an unsung skill in dealing with the plain, unvarnished people of Ireland. Many Irish Mammies and their kinfolk are the descendants of the people scattered to the bogs and mountains by Cromwell who venture out only to emigrate, see the Pope, sit in the audience of *Winning Streak* or go to a big match. And when they do venture out, they don't want to deal with a skinny-jeaned hipster who 'got his hair cut that way on purpose'. They want to talk to men and women who understand them, who can place a guiding arm around them to bring them closer to the mike, who can ask them if they want to say hello to anyone at home. They want to talk to someone like Marty Morrissey or Marty Whelan.

With Mícheál Ó Muircheartaigh off the air, to paraphrase the poet Austin Clarke, Marty is now the Sunday evening in every week. When he says, 'There won't be a cow milked in Clare tonght,' Irish Mammies and Himselves up and down the country chuckle, 'He's right you know,' and as the responsible farmers tear themselves away from the sweaty pubs to milk said cows, they know Marty feels their pain.

Whereas Marty M.'s domain is the great outdoors, the sun-bleached summer afternoons and the blustery showers outside a county-ground, Marty Whelan is the twinkly-eyed king of the studio.

A handy spin

The very randomness of the lottery selection process provides another opportunity to put the plain people of Ireland on television. And when Irish Mammies see the contestants on *Winning Streak*, they recognize them as their own.

There are thousands of euro up for grabs on the National Lottery game show but Irish Mammies and Himselves derive the most enjoyment from when Marty Whelan meets the contestants.

Even the startled but smiling contestants from the New Irish communities have a stronger Irish accent once they appear. 'How long have you been here, Olesegun?' 'Oh Lord, too long, Marty. Haha.'

'There's a fella from Senegal on tonight, if you don't mind,' say Irish Mammies. Or 'This girl is from the Ukraine – isn't she grand?'

But, by the law of averages, each show has to include at least one contestant from the mother lode. Tonight, it's Maureen from Roscommon. Tiny against the backdrop and the flashing lights, she confidently fields Marty Whelan's questions about the mascots.

'And who's this, Maureen?'

'That's a Dora doll. My granddaughter gave me that.'

'And Hannah Montana – would you be into her

yourself, Maureen?' asks Marty, playfully joshing, playing the role expected of him.

'No, no. Haha. I wouldn't know anything about Hannah Montana now indeed, Marty. Haha.'

'And tell me, is your granddaughter here with us tonight?' Marty asks, pushing the imaginary button which seems to deliver an electric shock to the interested parties in the studio audience. The camera cuts to a small child who is all too aware of the significance of her granny's next half an hour on this earth. It is all smiles in the group, but they will be heard swearing later if the money isn't big enough.

The guests press some buttons and win some prizes, until eventually it's time for the main event: Spin the Wheel. This time, the contestants are in competition with each other to match three symbols to get the chance to spin the wheel. A few minutes pass. Things hot up — a couple of contestants are now on two symbols. Whose ball is next? Oh, it's Maureen. 'She only needs one more symbol!' squeaks Irish Mammy at home as Maureen ponders whether the third symbol is concealed behind Light 1 or Light 5. The audience behind her is baying conflicting numbers as if their livelihoods depended on it.

'Five, Marty please,' says Maureen. There is a millisecond's pause. The earth seems stilled on its axis. The symbol behind Light 5 is revealed. It's a wheel. 'She has it,' says Irish Mammy — properly excited now on Maureen's behalf.

The studio lighting changes. The wheel is illuminated. It's a fiendishly simple concept, yet so powerful in its execution. Maureen totters up to it. She wears a bright-red suit. All glam. Marty directs her to her position.

Maureen has the process of spinning a wheel explained to her, and she grips it and gives it a whirl. The crowd roar at the bouncing ball. As it does every week, it flirts with one of the quarter-of-a-million slots before eventually settling at €15,000. The editors in the studio bring down the microphone channels on the audience briefly to reduce the chance of stifled 'For f**k sakes' as the minibus load of relatives realizes the cake is small and their slice good for nothing, only a few trips to Lidl.

Maureen seems happy with her lot. As does Irish Mammy: 'Fifteen thousand — isn't it enough for anyone too?'

A cautious reception

'Did one of ye move the aerial?... Ah why did ye go doing that? We had that set in a particular way.'

In September 2000, a seismic shift occurred in the TV-watching habits of Irish Mammies. Far away from the sitting rooms of the Irish hinterland, important discussions were taking place in a boardroom. *Coronation Street* was moving to TV3.

Now, suddenly, Weatherfield, which had until then been 'just a few miles down the road', had been transplanted to a strange land. For Irish Mammies without cable TV, relying on the rabbit ears, navigating to TV3 was not a straightforward business.

A daughter of one Irish Mammy, on arriving home for the weekend, was intrigued to spot a relatively recent-looking Spectra photo envelope. These envelopes — not so common now, since most photos never leave the digital camera — provided a useful record of what your parents might have been up to since you were last around.

In this case, the record showed that the parents had been taking photographs of the television. Puzzled, the daughter flicked through the entire package of snaps, and they consisted of almost identical photographs: the television in the sitting room with the aerial next to it. The one thing that linked the photographs was that they appeared to be all of the TV3 weather forecaster.

It was like a scene from a dark Scandinavian thriller.

> 'What's this?' Bjorglund asked the desk sergeant,
> who was regarding him with suspicion.
> 'Can't figure it out, just photographs of a
> weather forecaster.'
> 'Mind if I take a look?' Bjorglund leant in. His
> mind was racing. Where had he seen this before?
> Of course! Stockholm! The killer had struck again.
> Bjorglund needed another drink, badly.

Fortunately, this is not a psychological thriller, and Irish Mammy was on hand to provide the fiendishly simple explanation. 'We had fierce trouble getting TV3 in the sitting room for *Coronation Street* so I got your father to take photographs of where the aerial was when the reception was good. Be sure and put them back where you got them now, like a good girl.' Such lateral thinking will be lost for ever in the future, when the Internet is piped directly into our brains.

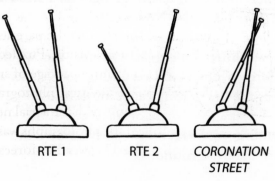

RTE 1   RTE 2   *CORONATION STREET*

Nationwide Building Society

By evening time, Irish Mammy is feeling battered by the media.

> ... the loss of some 100 jobs, which is a blow to the
> whole region ... the minister rejected accusations
> of stroke-politics, claiming his son was the best
> qualified for the job ... the victim was known to the
> gardai ... I mean, it's terrible, Joe, someone needs to
> do something about it, Joe ... the county board have
> confirmed that the talismanic centre forward has
> suffered cruciate ligament damage and will almost
> certainly miss the championship ... A spokesman
> for the bank said that they had no plans to cut
> interest rates ... later on tonight; a brand-new reality
> TV show begins: Take eight celebrities, an unusual
> situation, mayhem ensues! ...

Sigh. It's enough to make a Mammy crawl into a corner. But then shafts of celestial light break through the clouds. Norwegian band A-ha sang 'The Sun Always Shines on TV'. They must have been watching *Nationwide*. Outside the window, gale-force winds could be lifting roof slates and sending the firs swaying dangerously into the power lines, but the presenters of *Nationwide* still seem to be standing on the lawn of a stately home with azure skies in the background.

And it has Mary Kennedy. In the panoply of grand girls altogether, Mary is the grandest. She reads the news, speaks Irish, used to be a teacher, likes poems, presented the Eurovision without any giddiness. She even fronted afternoon television with Marty Whelan. She ticks all the boxes of Grand.

When she walks across the screen in the opening minutes of *Nationwide* and promises that later we will be meeting a retired missionary nun from Longford with a fascination for beekeeping, Irish Mammy knows everything is going to be all right.

In half an hour, there will be a return to misery. But, for now, we are a nation once again.

Ireland's got Mammies

As a race, the Irish were once shy; slow to seek attention, lest it be used against them as a sign of flightiness. 'Th'acting wasn't much good to him with the hay lying on the ground outside and the grass growing up through it.' Only a few went in for that sort of thing — they were the Showpeople. They had a licence to be acting, even if it was just acting the maggot.

Now we are all showpeople. Fly-on-the-wall talent-competition TV is pervasive; Making a Show of Yourself is now a good thing. To support this level of omigod-I-got-through-to-the-Judge's-House, tears and general drama, the Irish Mammy has been thrust into the spotlight and become Show Mammy. In the past, a Show Mammy was just standing in the Hall, responding to school-concert-related emergencies: 'What's the matter peitin? ... What wings? ... You never said you needed wings ... Which bit? ... What "fantasy sequence"? ... Look, I've a bit of wire netting in the boot and an oul table cloth. We'll make some sort of wings for you ... Stop crying now, darling.'

Now she has had to do it all in front of the cameras. She is there hugging the crying/laughing contestant after the (un)successful audition, worrying about the state of the place when the production team come calling for the Bootcamp Bit or giving out stink about criticism levelled at her child on the weight-loss show *Operation Transformation*.

'Carly is only doing her best. That nutritionist had no right saying what she said.'

As the mood of the contestant's family rises and falls through the programme, Show Mammy has to stay constant and on-message. Showbusiness is a harsh world.

I don't know. I think she's some sort of celebrity

There's reality TV, and then there's reality TV.

In the main, the trials and tribulations of ersatz celebrities doing mediocre things across all channels would leave many Irish Mammies comfortably numb. There is the brief recognition factor and a slight thrill at seeing a familiar figure outside their normal environment, like seeing one of their children's teachers in SuperValu. It soon wears off though, and they claim they're 'only half-looking at it, to tell you the truth'.

Then there are those other programmes, where shiny young things who want to be ersatz celebrities are put through their humiliating paces.

If they happen to stumble across one of these programmes on their way to the news and weather or while trying to escape the quare film, they may pause to ponder the inhumanity of it all.

Every so often there comes an antidote to this — like *ICA** *Bootcamp*. Perhaps one of the producers of the programme had been sitting next to their mother on the couch as they both accidentally watched the latest episode of *Young, Horny and Completely without Shame* and heard her tut.

Because *ICA Bootcamp* has everything an Irish Mammy could wish for. It looks a bit like *Nationwide*, apart from the lack of sunshine. It has young wans that could learn a thing or two and a phalanx of fine respectable women to teach them.

Most importantly, the show contains cows and hens, two animals Irish Mammies feel an affinity with. Like them, despite all they've been through, cows and hens just get on with it.

---

*ICA — Irish Countrywoman's Association — a sort of MBA programme for Irish Mammies.

7

I Will, Faith

If you were as good at saying your prayers as you
are at answering back...

Mass

There is a murmur: 'It's Himself tonight.' When an Irish Mammy of the Mass-attending variety refers to a Himself in the context of which priest is on tonight, she is more than likely referring to the Parish Priest. The 'Himself' will be accompanied by a slight raise of the eyes to heaven — as if sharing a joke with Himself's boss — and a little smile. It's the smile that is reserved by Irish Mammies in the presence of men who have a position of authority on paper although the real work is done elsewhere.

'Not a bad evening, Father.'

'Not a bad evening at all, Mrs Flynn. A bit of daylight this evening. We soon won't want any lights.'

'No, indeed, Father. No lights is right, just-then.'

'Now, let me see, the missal is out, is it?'

'The missal is out, Father. 'Tis all set up. As the fella said, the stage is set.'

'Fair play to you, Susan. You're a mighty organizer altogether. We'd be lost without you, hah?'

'Arra, I'm sure ye'd be grand, Father. 'Tis only a few bits and pieces.'

Despite all that's happened, in parishes up and down the country, Irish Mammies are in the vanguard of looking after the little bits and pieces that keep the Church ticking over. It's not easy to keep doing so. Many have deep misgivings about the Church's cover-ups and lack of charity in its treatment of women, children, the vulnerable and the different. Some gave up on Mass completely. Those Irish Mammies that still help out in church do so as an expression of their own spirituality, community spirit and in solidarity with the 'sound' priests rather than any loyalty to 'some of them oul yokes in the Vatican … and their oul new Mass.'

Apart from the odd hiccup, Mass continues on as normal. The lads doing the collection shuffle awkwardly up the side, uncomfortable in the attention. They'll slip out a whispered 'How's Paddy?' to a familiar face if they're sitting on the edge of the row, as the plate is fed into the pews like a rugby ball into a scrum. Men lean and contort, half standing as they scrabble in their back pockets for a two-euro coin, but Irish Mammy has the correct and appropriate amount in her purse ready, plus extra for any curve balls presented by the time of year — petrol collections, November masses, St Vincent de Paul, the Missions. As Roy Keane might say, 'Fail to prepare, Prepare to be caught out by a second collection.'

Indeed, priests have been known to be reminded about the second collection by seeing the disappointed looks of Mammies who are poised to donate.

The Mass proceeds to the 'The peace of the Lord be with you always. / And also with you' section, as the congregation tries to remember whether 'this fella' is a priest who 'does the shake hands' or does not. They flinch in anticipation of touching their neighbour. They are further discommoded because 'And also with you' has been changed to 'And with your spirit.' As if the situation wasn't tense enough.

The settlement pattern of the Mass is shown overleaf. The lines — 'isomammies' — join regions of similar Mammies.

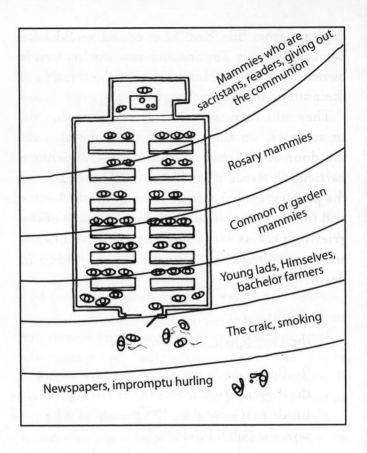

Mammies who are sacristans, readers, giving out the communion

Rosary mammies

Common or garden mammies

Young lads, Himselves, bachelor farmers

The craic, smoking

Newspapers, impromptu hurling

That'll be a big funeral

On big feast days, gathered outside the church will be lads who are technically at Mass, having gone in to bless themselves, but to all intents and purposes are just people standing outside a building. In days gone by, this kind of a crowd would have been there every Sunday, but now having finally owned up to their Mammies that they don't go, their attendance record is patchy.

They still turn up for funerals, though, and in summer, on the night of the removal, with the door of the church open, you experience a particularly Irish phenomenon. The sound of the prayers inside becomes mixed with the banter and the laughing outside, as if every aspect of the grieving process — the loss and the memories — are blended together in a soundscape of life and death.

'The third glorious mystery: The descent of the Holy Spirit. Our Father ...'

'It slipped down the hill and next of all wasn't the digger shtuck inside in the river, Johnny inside in it — balubas. Get me out of it he says, the pub'll be closing.'

Laughter.

'Blessed is the fruit of thy womb, Jesus ...'

'By Jayz, he'd go anywhere for a match — I remember wan day I met him thumbing back along. I gave him a lift. Where'r oo going Johnny? Says he, "I'm going to watch th'under-21s training." "Training?" I says.

Says he, "They'll have a puckaround at the end." Chrisht, he was some character.[*]

Back at the rosary, where the rest of the congregation falters, a core of elite prayer-ers take over to shore up the saying of the kind of prayers everyone has forgotten. These are prayers that undulate on the kind of language you won't see uttered in accompaniment to any Kumbaya-style guitar-led hymn: 'exile', 'valley of tears', 'banished children of Eve' — phrases more likely now to be used as the title of a Booker-prize-winning novel set in a desert town in the American Midwest exploring the dark heart of the human psyche, than in any modern prayer.

When there are 'Hail, Holy Queens' and other rosary-related prayers to be said, Irish Mammies drift into the lead with the inexorable progress of East Africans in a middle-distance race. The

---

[*] The Character exists in every Irish town. Maybe he is a man called 'The Yank', who has no affiliation at all with the United States but always wears a cowboy hat. Sometimes 'character' may be a peculiarly Irish euphemism to describe a raving alcoholic or complete lunatic. Saddam Hussein would be called a character. If Saddam Hussein had been buried at an Irish country funeral, it would have been a most picaresque tableau, with an interesting clash of cultures: members of his al-Begat tribe ululating at the front while, down the back, the locals, including Irish Mammies, saying things like 'Didn't he go very sudden in the end?' and 'I hear it's the sister will get the house.'

Europeans fade away, and by the time 'we may imitate what they contain and obtain what they promise' comes, it's just Irish Mammies loping comfortably out in front, unflustered.

Mammies know what to do at funerals — what to say; when it is appropriate to say it was 'a blessing he was taken without any pain'; and when to say nothing. The lads at the back will focus on the practicalities.

> 'The family said to come away back to Con Twomey's after the graveyard. There's a big spread put on there, I'm told.'

A grave situation

Funerals are a time for contemplation and, as Mammy and Himself get older, thoughts turn to their own 'arrangements'.

> 'I'll let you go anyway, peitin. I don't want to be using up your credit.'

> 'That's all right, Mammy. I get free calls at weekends. So you've no more news?'

> 'Nothing else strange now ... Let me see ... oh, we bought a plot too.'

'What?!'

'Well, you remember your father wanted to be buried with his own people? I can understand that. But, says I, 'Who's going to visit us halfway up a mountain?' And neither would I ask them to. But he was quite adamant, so I said no more about it.'

'And what happened?'

'Well, it must have been after Nancy Corrigan's funeral ...'

'Nancy Corrigan died?'

'Oh, she did. I thought I told you that ... Ah, she was bad for a good while. Dementia in the end, the poor thing ... Anyway, it was a beautiful dry day and the graveyard was looking lovely. They'd done a fine job on it. And on our way home, out of the blue, didn't your father say: "Do you know something, I wouldn't mind being buried in this place?" I didn't say anything much at the time. I just let it sit there, and the following day he said it again, so I said, "Right, we'd better move fast." Off in with us to the Council and, to cut a long story short, didn't we get a lovely plot altogether, not too far from the gate.'

'So ye're happy with that?'

'Oh, we are. And do you know who's next to us?'

'No. Who?'

'Patsy Tallon — isn't that a good one?!'

'Who's Patsy Tallon?'

'Ah, you *know* him all right. Died a good while ago. He used to drive a green van. Gave you a lollipop one time. Ah you *do* know him.'

'… I suppose …'

'Well, poor Patsy is on our left, and Dr Tim Dooley — would you believe? — is on our right. So we'll be in good company.'

That'll do us grand.

8

Get That Into You Now

Will you have it in a bowl or with a wafer?

Tea …

One cannot overstate the importance of being able to make the tea properly – particularly for the Visitor.

The Irish Mammy, needless to say, is synonymous with the ritual of suggesting, cajoling, ah-you-willing, bustling around, rustling up a packet of biscuits that are the prelude to the arrival of the tea.

The Mammy accomplishes all of this while simultaneously extracting information. The barrage is relentless; as if in a game of tennis, the visitor will furiously try to bat back, but Irish Mammy will play a variety of shots to bamboozle the guest before eventually smashing a forehand passing shot down the line.

Irish Mammy to serve:

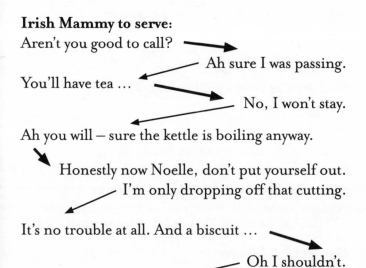

Aren't you good to call?

Ah sure I was passing.

You'll have tea …

No, I won't stay.

Ah you will – sure the kettle is boiling anyway.

Honestly now Noelle, don't put yourself out. I'm only dropping off that cutting.

It's no trouble at all. And a biscuit …

Oh I shouldn't.

How're they all?

Grand altogether.

Sugar?

No thanks, just a drop of milk.

And how's Mike in Missouri?

Flying it.

Would you eat a scone if I warmed it up?

I don't know, I'm supposed to be minding myself.

Engineering, isn't he?

That's right. Engineering.

Ah you'll have a scone. They're just made.

I will, sure.

Engineering's a good thing to be in, faith.

'Tis surely.

A good thing. I'll get you some jam.

Don't trouble yourself at all Noelle.

And does he have a girlfriend out there?

No he doesn't. He says he doesn't have time.

The Americans work them hard indeed.
Are you ready for a hot drop? And you might as well have a few biscuits as well. They're bourbons.

[Sighs] I will so. You're an awful woman, Noelle.

Game: Irish Mammy.

116

... and sandwiches

To truly appreciate Mammies in action, one needs to go to a function. When a group of Mammies converge *en masse* at a do in the hall, armed with sandwiches, buns and tea, it is a sight to behold. This is tea-making on an industrial scale, and the conversation is even further compressed.

> *Tea, Mrs Cooney? You will. Milk and sugar over there. What-about-this-boy-what'll-you-have? A bun, is it? What do you say? Good boy. Take your bun now. Will he have a drop of Fanta? What about you, Mrs Nolan? Tea. Of course you can. Oh, we've a load of sandwiches. Salad. Ham. Egg. Which one? Egg. There you go now, Mrs Nolan. And Tess? Coffee???! Oh right, let me see ...*

It is typical of the male-centric account that Jesus's carry-on with the loaves and fishes in the Bible makes no mention of the real miracle: how all that food was distributed to the hungry thousands. There must have been Irish Mammies in the supply chain.

Irish Mammy: What'll you have, Mrs Zechariah? Fish. And you'll have a loaf? Oh, the Lord save us, I completely forgot, Mrs Zechariah, shur you're a coeliac. I'm sorry.

Did you ever see such a crowd, Mary? *No* preparation at all of course, and they expecting the likes of *you and me* to work miracles here. Only for Sarah Hartigan bringing the baskets for the scraps. We'd be lost only for her. Says she, 'I thought I was mad bringing these, and we only have two loaves and five fish, but I says, I might as well.' What about yourself, Johnny? Loaf. Right you are, Johnny. Butter and marmalade over there.

Jesus (*wandering over, looking pleased with himself*): Ye're doing great work here altogether, Bridget, The back-room team. Hah?

Irish Mammy: Oh sure, you know yourself. The show must go on.

The catering teapot

None of this is possible without Irish Mammy's best friend: the catering teapot. If the catering for a large group of people needs to be done with military precision, then the catering teapot is the Kalashnikov of Irish Mammyhood: lightweight, easy to hold and capable of rapid, sustained use without the need of reloading. It also has an efficient German feel to it — the catering teapot is an object Mammies can trust.

Mämmi

Vorsprung durch Tea

Perfectly good food

Much has been written about the potato and Ireland.

Irish Mammy knows all about the potato. Yes, it is true there is nothing like the humble spud, but take your eye off it for a second when it's boiling and tragedy ensues.

'She rang and I doing the dinner. Half of them fell apart in the pot and then the rest are hard in the middle. These spuds'd break your heart.'

But there is another round vegetable that requires

no such minding. The turnip. You never hear of the Great Turnip Famine. Why not? Because that's not how turnips roll. Irish Mammy knows that. German Mammies know that. The winter of 1916–17 is called the Turnip Winter in Germany because turnips kept the population alive when the effete potatoes had been killed by an early frost.

Along with 60 per cent tax rates, elbow patches on your school jumper and Theresa Lowe's *Where in the World*, the turnip was one of the things that made this country great.

Even though peeling them was like trying to shear a slippery, vegetabular sheep, Mammies wrestled with turnips because she knew that, along with the spuds and a few peas, they'd form a protective tricolour that would keep the family from the workhouse until the next Big Shop.

Turnips never get the glory afforded to more glamorous colleagues. There are no hand-cooked crisps made out of turnips. No artisan turnip products have faux-vintage packaging with a quote from a farmer on it. Turnips have an image problem: a colour scheme like an alcoholic's nose, an unremarkable shape and, of course, turnips have a slight BO problem. 'Boil a turnip and the whole world knows about it …' goes the relatively new saying.

At some stage around the turn of the millennium, we rejected what Mammy and the turnip had done for us. We turned our back on it, sometimes in favour of celeriac. If ever a vegetable was promoted beyond its ability, it's celeriac. Its very name sounds like it has a food intolerance to itself.

Now that we're humbler, and listening to Mammy again, the day of the turnip has returned.

Everyone's brown bread is different but what I do is ...

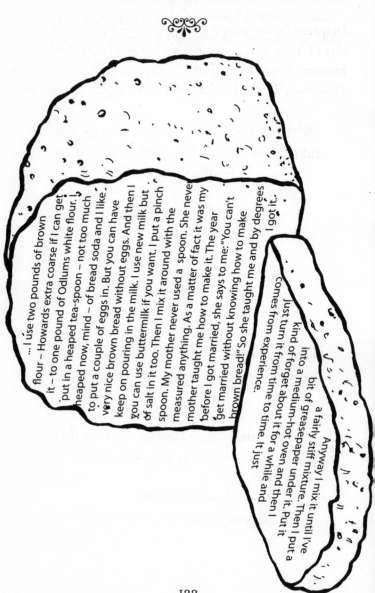

... I use two pounds of brown flour – Howards extra coarse if I can get it – to one pound of Odlums white flour. I put in a heaped tea-spoon – not too much heaped now, mind – of bread soda and I like to put a couple of eggs in. But you can have very nice brown bread without eggs. And then I you can use buttermilk if you want. I put a pinch keep on pouring in the milk. I use new milk but of salt in it too. Then I mix it around with the spoon. My mother never used a spoon. She neve measured anything. As a matter of fact it was my mother taught me how to make it. The year before I got married, she says to me: "You can't get married without knowing how to make brown bread!" So she taught me and by degrees I got it.

Anyway I mix it until I've into a medium-hot oven under it. Put it bit of greasepaper under it. Then I put a kind of forget about it for a while and then I just turn it comes from time to time. It just a fairly stiff mixture.

A meal. That'll be lovely

Inspired by the movie *When Harry Met Sally* but without any of 'that' carry-on, here's a scene from the little-known film *When Irish Mammy and Himself Said to Themselves, 'Do You Know Something, We Might Go for a Meal.'*

SCENE: A RESTAURANT, NOTHING TOO FANCY, MIND. A WAITRESS IS TAKING IRISH MAMMY AND HIMSELF'S ORDER.

Waitress:
Would you like to order some drinks?

Himself:
Hah?

Irish Mammy:
Drinks, Gerry. She's asking if you'd like to have something to drink with your dinner.

Himself:
Oh bedads — I don't know. What do they have on offer?

Irish Mammy:
Maybe you'd like a Cidona?

Himself:

Oh, a Cidona. That'll be grand …

Irish Mammy:

Now, Gerry, what do you want for a starter?

Himself:

Oh, are we having starters too? This is a mighty spread altogether. What are the choices?

Irish Mammy:

Well, they've vol-o-vongs. It's a sort of chicken and mushroom pastry.

Himself:

That sounds nice. I might have one of those maybe.

Irish Mammy:

You don't eat mushrooms though.

Himself:

Don't I?

Irish Mammy:

No, they give you indigestion. Do you remember you went through nearly a box of Rennie that last time?

Himself:

I'll keep away from them so.

Irish Mammy:

Why don't you have the soup? You always go for the soup. I think I might have the prawn cocktail … And I suppose you'll have the beef for the main course?

Himself:

I will I s'pose. What comes with it?

Irish Mammy (*reading*):

Roast beef with jus of red wine and roasted shallots, pureed celeriac.

Himself:

What kind of a yoke is a celeriac?

Irish Mammy:

Some sort of a turnip, I think. Shur, if you don't like it, you can leave it to one side.

(*addressing the waitress*)

Could we have the soup and the beef, and I'll have the prawn cocktail and the salmon.

CUT TO THE END OF THE DINNER. THERE ARE
TWO EMPTY PLATES IN FRONT OF THEM.

Irish Mammy:
You ate the celeriac away.

Himself:
I did, mind you. It wasn't bad at all.

THE WAITRESS ARRIVES.

Waitress:
Something for dessert?

Irish Mammy:
Well, I know what I want anyway. I'll have
the pavlova.*

---

*In the field of psychology, it is a common misconception that the phrase 'Pavlovian response' originates from Pavlov's observation that his dogs would salivate in anticipation of food before they received it. In fact, Pavlovian response is the automatic choice by an Irish Mammy of the pavlova as soon as she sees it on a menu, or sees someone else having it.

Christmas every day

'Now what would ye like next? Another bitta-cake or a biscuit, or maybe a Milk Tray? I've the plum pudding on as well. Are the selection boxes open yet? Why don't ye open up one there while ye're waiting?'

'Mammy, sit down and relax for yourself.'

Mammy makes a noise that's halfway between a snort and an ironic laugh. Relax? Around Christmas? The very thought.

Today is the culmination of a year. No one does Christmas like an Irish Mammy. Far away from the big gestures favoured by the Himselves — the Christmas tree, the lights on the lawn — Mammy's Christmas starts the previous St Stephen's Day.

The 12 Months of Christmas

Task	J	F	M	A	M	J	J	A	S	O	N	D	25
Worry were the plates hot enough	█												
Say you had 'a quiet Christmas'		█											
Freeze the Christmas cake			█										
Remember there's a Christmas cake in the freezer				█									
Become fed up of that oul Christmas cake					█								
Get started on the Christmas cake							█						
Go back for glacé cherries								█					
Confirm child homecoming dates								█					
Decide that the book being promoted on the *Late Late Show* will be your present from Himself									█				
Say 'don't be talking to me' when Fran Carrigan asks if you are 'all set for The Christmas?'										█			
Cut the postage deadlines out of the paper and put on door of press										█			
Send Christmas cards											█		
Big Shop											█		
Secondary Big Shop												█	
Third Big Shop: 'I thought I only had to pick up a few things but it came to well over €100 in the end'												█	
Order the turkey							█						
'There's no way that turkey was 14 pounds'													█
'Look, take him one of the boxes of Roses. We won't eat them at all'													█

9

They Grow Up So Fast

Have a bit of patience and I'll get it for you
now in a second.

Though the children have left, Irish Mammy is not finished. She may have taken her retirement from the Rearing Children Department of the Public Service, however, like all public service redundancy schemes, within minutes, she is swiftly rehired as a consultant.

Flat craic

Irish sons can be notoriously useless once they have left the nest. Here — in flat-pack technology — is what happens next.

SAÛSSPÅN

Addressing the situation

If you look at an Irish Mammy's address book, her children's path through life, as well as the economic health of the country, is traced out simply and succinctly.

She was nursing above in Dublin for a while and didn't she get an offer to go out to Dubai, would you believe? Next thing I hear she's met this fella. An engineer of some sort, and they came back home. Big wedding, the whole shebang. Then it got very quiet for him and the whole lot of them are gone out to Australia. 'Twill be two years this March.

Pushing the envelope

If there are addresses, there must be letters that need to be readdressed. Over time, the number of letters that need addressing gradually reduces. Which is a pity, because the tradition of passing on messages on the outside of them may die out. And they can be a handy carrier pigeon to bring further messages out of the homestead — messages that are hopefully only intelligible to the recipient.

Share options

Irish Mammy and Himself are up visiting the Eldest in Dublin.

Standing in his kitchen, the Eldest is on edge in case any of his flatmates arrive downstairs.

> 'Who's here at the moment?' says Mammy, as if guessing his thoughts.

> 'Gaz ... I mean Gary and Bernadette.'

> 'Bernadette is the —'

> 'The Brazilian girl, yes.'

> ''Tis all very exotic here,' adds Himself.

> 'I suppose they were out socializing last night,' says Mammy.

> 'They were, yes,' says the Eldest, recalling in horror that he was woken at 4 a.m. by the sound of 'The Gazinator' making tea and toast for a girl. This sound, as it turned out, was an essential prelude to some other sounds that the Eldest heard later, and he lay awake praying they would not feel the urge to make those sounds again for his parents to hear. The door opens.

'Oh, so sorry,' says Bernadette, dressed in a silk nightgown which is covered in a print of a large dragon. 'I forgot your parents, they come this morning.'

'Don't be apologizing at all. Shur, we're the ones who are putting you out,' says Mammy, wearing a 'So this is the famous Bernadette' expression on her face.

'Oh, haha – thank you. You are not putting me out. So you are going to see some of Dublin today?'

'Oh, this lad has a full programme of events planned for us.'

'Remember I was saying Bernadette's an artist. That's one of her paintings there,' says the Eldest proudly, pointing at the wall.

'Most unusual – lovely colours,' says Mammy. 'A sort of seascape, is it?'

'It is supposed to be a picture of my mind after I came here to Ireland,' explains Bernadette. 'So I guess like the sea, changing, sometime peaceful, sometimes stormy.'

'Oh, isn't it great to be artistic. I was never any good at that,' says Mammy.

'Yes, but pay not so good,' giggles Bernadette.

'Oh shur I know, but as long as you are doing what makes you happy, that's all that matters.'

The Eldest is astonished. This philosophy doesn't tally at all with Irish Mammy's previous statements like: 'Oh, for goodness' sake, can't you stick at it at least until you get your degree?'

But he is not aware of the Irish Mammy tradition that exploring different theories on the pursuit of happiness should only be applied to other people's children.

'Thank you – I think so, yes. Maybe I ask you to say that to my mother.'

'Oh, now, Bernadette, I'm sure she's very proud ... Would you believe, the first ever film I saw at the pictures was called *Song of Bernadette*. It's about Lourdes; you know.'

'Oh yes, my mother named me after Bernadette ... yes ...'

'Is that right? 'Magine. Isn't that a good one?'

Now it's Irish Mammy's turn to be lost in thought. She is far away, sitting on a verandah in Brazil, sipping tea and chatting to Bernadette's mother about pilgrimages.

'I suppose we'd better go.' The Eldest is first to shake the trio out of their Bernadette-inspired reverie.

Irish Mammy spots a problem.

'Are they the jeans you are wearing?'

Irish Mammies have the unique capability to raise existential questions about a pair of jeans.

'What's wrong with them?'

'Ah now …' Irish Mammy shares a conspiratorial glance with Bernadette, who is laughing.

'I'll be relying on you now, Bernadette, to keep an eye on this fella for me. Can't even dress himself properly.'

Later that day, Mammy has had time to think and is pronouncing her judgement.

'Bernadette seems like a grand girl. A bit "alternative", you know, but a fine sensible girl all the same.'

Between the lines

No matter what age the Mammy or the child, there will always be moments of mutual misunderstanding.

For the child of any age, it may be useful to consult a primer outlining what Mammy thinks on a number of topics.

Opposite is a cut-out-and-keep cheat-sheet that should help you navigate a large proportion of Mammy-related situations.

What is she like at all? Mammy.....

...didn't let on of course but thinks herself that:	...wishes you wouldn't:	...wonders if it wouldn't be more in your line to:
She could have left the socializing alone for one night.	Crack your knuckles, you know it gets on her nerves.	Finish up your spuds and don't mind your whining?
That dress was a bit short.	Be telling all and sundry about it.	Be saying your prayers than to be looking around you?
He's getting very jowly.	Be picking at that scab on your knee. It'll heal in its own good time.	Be studying for your exam than to be at that oul computer?
They could have made an effort to be here for the dinner but they were 'busy' no doubt.	Go out again tonight. Can't you stay in and take it easy?	Settle down now. Haven't you enough gallivanting?
They took their time baptizing that child.	Be playing that thing at the table.	Mind your money than to be getting a new sofa and the old one barely used?

The Grammy

Many Irish Mammies are now grandmothers themselves. This has ushered in a glorious new era of lower-worry childcare; where they can in most cases hand back their grandchild at the end of the day — but not before extracting some crucial information and experience about the modern world which can be used in future natters with their fellow Grammies.

IO

Gone Away Somewhere

Arrived safely tg 27dgs love to all xx

Stranded

It may seem hard to believe, now that Climate Change – or as it's known in this country, More Rain – has decommissioned our summers, but there are people in Ireland who remember good weather. Those sun-drenched memories started the night before, with the making of the Holiday Sandwiches, containing exotic fillings and cut with an extra flourish. Cheese singles, which tasted like a by-product of the petrochemical rather than the dairy industry, were put to one side. It was a time for renewal and sandwiches containing the likes of scallions and ham.

The familiar bottles of salad cream and Thousand Island dressing were decanted into little pots. A 500ml bottle of TK White Lemonade, its packaging and labels long gone, would carry the milk. Tomorrow they would be going on a magical journey.

Everyone was up early the following morning – the forecast said there'd be rain in the afternoon, so it was important to get the good bit of the day. Mammy was long up, looking girlish – having thrown caution to the wind and worn the white trousers with a white cardigan.

'Oh, you'd no more look at them and they'd be dirty.'

This was not a day for caution — it was a day for the seaside and unexpected treats and parents not wearing sensible clothes. (Although she has not completely lost it — clinging like a joey in a pouch, there are still tissues somewhere in the sleeve of the cardigan.)

Then the children squeezed into the car. There were no rear seatbelts but luckily families were larger, so there were enough children to provide quite a tight wedge of child in the back seat that did much the same job as a seatbelt. The combination of tight squeeze, sticky heat and short trousers meant that when the family reached the destination, the children exited the back seat with a series of pleasing *shlump* sounds as they peeled themselves off the leatherette. Some families had enough for a second tier of children. When they emerged blinking into the sunlight, the lower tier rubbed the feeling back into their thighs after a couple of hours of being bruised by a younger sibling's bony arse.

That was if the car made it to the seaside. Mammies had to be highly skilled in expectation management, because there was always a risk the car would break down. Once the car had slid to an anti-climactic halt miles from the sea and Himself had gone to look for a phone box, someone had to stay behind and break the news.

Most of the time, the car managed to retain the use of its vital organs for one more journey, and a child was able to retain a little innocence and not hear the awful phrase, 'It's the alternator, mate, she's gone.'

The seaside of the past was a different seaside to now. There were no kite-surfers with their ruddy good health and optimism to make you feel guilty for not 'living life to the max', no farmer's markets to intercept you with crackers and dips and anti-oxidants. It was a democratic place where all were equal in the eyes of the sun. Because it was 100 per cent Irish, it was also a haven for all that was gloriously lumpy and blotched about the human form. You couldn't get body dysmorphia on an Irish beach as you performed the stumbling dance of togging out.

'Are you coming in, Mammy?'

'I might dip my toes later. Don't go out too far now.'

Irish Mammy took up position, digging into a beach head and minding everything while she read *The Lilac Bus*, one eye scanning the horizon.

And then suddenly she decided to take the plunge! An Institution was now wearing a swimming costume and being … giddy. This was a moment to remember.

Afterwards, there was a hunger like no other for the sandwiches, with the white bread nicely squashed so that it was impossible to tell where bread ended and the filling began. The cups of tea were drunk, the cups rinsed in and then filled with TK, and the crisps – by now almost crushed to powder – were eaten, every so often with a slight extra crunch as sand made its way into the mouth. Then Irish Mammy took out money for chips. What's got into her?

On the car journey home, the children sniffed the burnt smell of their arms, looked at the white strip where their watch used to be. They of course forgot the Irish Tanning Graph, which says that the Peak of New Tan is followed by the Trough of Peeling. It didn't matter. For now, they were Swiss Family Robinson.

The day was complete and, tired but happy, the family prepared for bed.

'You'll sleep tonight, after all the sea air.'

Snap out of it

One thing that is sadly in decline now is the classic photo of the Irish Mammy.

It was one of the family, taken by Himself, standing 50 yards away with a camera that looked like it shouldn't work at all. Mammy would protest severely that she hated having her photo taken, and would hide behind a clutch of children.

But these snaps are real. They are somewhere in a box. They can be held and passed around in all their fading glory. All the closed eyes and missing heads and feet, all the blurry, shaky, squinting sun ones, all the self-timer ones where nobody knows

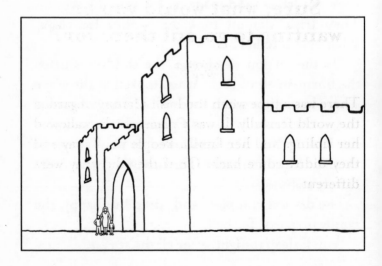

when the timer is going to go off. They are all inside The Box. Even though these imperfect images caused a groan when they were first thumbed through outside the chemist, now they seem just as important as the perfect shots. Perhaps because they tell a little more about the person taking the picture.

These photos are no more now. There has been a huge explosion of narcissism in this country, sparked by Facebook, camera phones and an improvement in general skin quality caused by the introduction of smoothies. As a result, no one is afraid of getting their photo taken any more.

Sure, what would you be wanting to go out there for?

There was a time when the Irish Mammy regarded the world fearfully. It was a place which swallowed her siblings and her family. People went away and they didn't come back. Or if they did they were different.

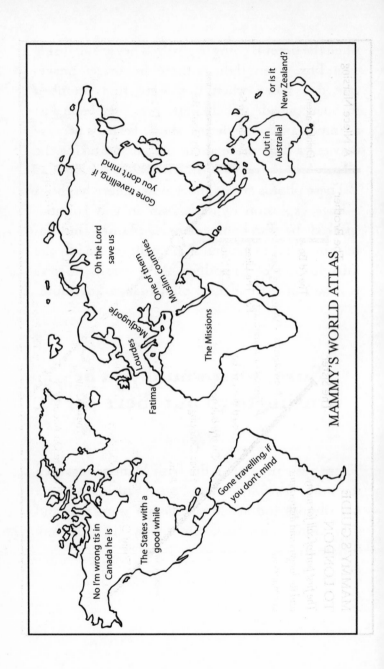

MAMMY'S WORLD ATLAS

Out in
Australia!

or is it
New Zealand?

Gone travelling, if
you don't mind

Oh the Lord
save us

One of them
Muslim countries

Medjugorje

Lourdes

Fatima

The Missions

No I'm wrong tis in
Canada he is

The States with a
good while

Gone travelling, if
you don't mind

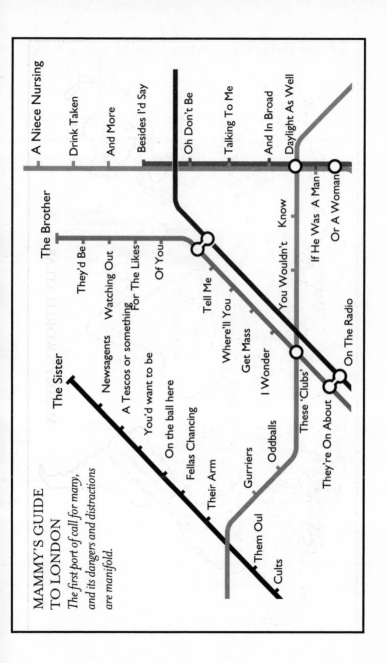

MAMMY'S GUIDE
TO LONDON
*The first port of call for many,
and its dangers and distractions
are manifold.*

The Sister

Cults
Them Oul
Their Arm
Fellas Chancing
On the ball here
You'd want to be
A Tescos or something
Newsagents
Watching Out
They'd Be

The Brother

Of You
For The Likes

Oddballs
Gurriers
I Wonder
Get Mass
Where'll You
Tell Me

These 'Clubs'
They're On About
On The Radio
You Wouldn't Know
If He Was A Man
Or A Woman

A Niece Nursing
Drink Taken
And More
Besides I'd Say
Oh Don't Be
Talking To Me
And In Broad
Daylight As Well

149

If we don't go now, we'll never go

Irish Mammies are on the move. Whether visiting their children or just going on adventures, the world is opening up. Places that seemed inaccessible are now their playground.

II

Neighbourhood Watch

You needn't be saying that around the road now.

You can tell when there are lots of Mammies in the area. The community has a different feel. The Irish Mammies are like the eggs in the brown bread, subtly giving the area a softer texture and holding it more tightly together. They are to be seen bustling around with half the under-14s in the back of a people carrier on the way to a League semi-final against a hated rival district; they are Walking the Road, arms swinging, clad in fleeces; they are stopped in conversation, asking for the latest news on ailments, spouses and children; they are leaning on the gate, waylaying passing walkers by putting talk on them.

They are around. Stop your messing.

What was I going to say again …?

List of useful things to say to facilitate continuity in conversation

- So that's the way.

- Wait till I see if I've any more news.

- Go *wan*!

- Go *way*!

- Isn't *that* a good one?

- So that was grand.*

- Oh, I know, shur.

- Sure, who are you telling?

- Ah, that's more of it now.

- And where are they now?†

---

*'So that was grand' is an extremely useful conjunction to allow a longer form of narrative to proceed from one stage to another. It does not imply that 'that' actually was 'grand'. In fact, taken in isolation, 'that' can be anything but grand, but compared to what's about to come next in the plot, 'that' is relatively benign. It also signals to the listener that 'that' is not the main point of the story. For example: 'He told me: Three thousand euro to replace the carpets ... But anyway so that was grand. Then he starts telling me how much it's going to cost to fix the walls.'

†Implying, what are the children of that family doing now? The continued fecundity of the Irish population means families are still comparatively larger than those in the rest of Europe, so an itemization of the activities of a family, *particularly* if any of them became solicitors, doctors or nurses, may take some time.

The bus

*'Here's the bus now. Bang on time he is too,
mind you.'*

Some Irish Mammies will be lucky to live in an area with some sort of public transport. In both rural and urban areas, a busload of Irish Mammies on their way to Town is a sight and sound to behold.

As the bus proceeds towards the city centre, the Mammy quotient increases until, by the time it reaches the destination, it has become a cacophony of News.

'Hello, Bernie. You're down the back of the bus this time.'

'I know. Like the bold boys.'

'Isn't it very crowded this morning?'

'Ash Wednesday, I suppose. All going in to get the Ashes.'

'I doubt that then. The shops, more like it, haha. What time are you coming home again?'

'Oh, I'll get the quarter past one — I don't want to be knocked over by the young lads.'

Bus-Mammies inhabit the daylight in between the rush hours. The other buses are too loud, the queue too disorderly, as teenagers form a scrum to get to important seats next to other teenagers they fancy or want to emulate.

Neither would you find many Mammies on the Late Bus — the province of cramming students and, in rural areas, the true apotheosis of the Irish drinker — The Man Who Wanted to Talk to the Driver (see Chapter 13: Roadworthy).

No, the in-between bus is best.

Whether it's the movement of the bus, the knowledge that there is only a limited time, or the chance that the gossip might be interrupted by some other latchico sitting down in the seat next to them, Mammies are in full interrogation flight.

*Mrs Kenny was on the bus. Of course. Wanted to know all about you. Says she, 'IS THE DAUGHTER STILL IN ABU DHABI?' And, you know, of course, she's as deaf as a beetle so she was as **loud**. The whole bus must have heard.*

Anyway, 'No,' says I. 'She's back from there a good while.'

IS SHE MARRIED YET says she. I said you were, to a man from Clare. ('Tis Clare Fergal is from, isn't it? ... Clare, yes.)

CLARE? says she. HAD SHE TO GO ALL

*THE WAY OVER THERE LOOKING FOR A
MAN?* Oh, she's such a character. I didn't mind. I
knew she was half-codding. That's just her 'way'.

Then that was grand and the bus picked up Lily
Fitzpatrick. Of course she made a beeline for me.

'I haven't seen you in ages,' says she, and of course
she wanted all the news. 'Is it your girl is working
for the Arabs?' says she, so I had to tell her your
story. 'I suppose she's on the big money,' says she.

Of course I didn't let on I knew anything.

'Oh, shur, she tells me nothing,' I says.

I'm telling you, you'd want your wits about you on
that bus.

NEARLY FROM THE DOOR – FINE - AND - HANDY FOR YOURSELF – INTO TOWN 434

MONDAY TO SATURDAY

SERVICE NUMBER	434	434	434	434	434
The Crossroads below (dep.)	08:00	10:00	13:00	17:00	20:00
Over by Nan Sullivans	08:07	10:07			
The new flyover	08:15	10:15	13:15	17:15	20:15
Across from the Topaz	08:24	10:24	13:24	17:24	20:24
Not too far awayno... no indeed...					
true for you Mrs Phelan	08:38	10:38	13:38	17:38	20:38
Town (The Tech)	08:50	10:50	13:50	17:50	20:50
Town (Mass for the First Friday)	08:55	10:55	13:55	17:55	20:55
Town (SuperValu) (arr.)	09:00	11:00	14:00	18:00	21:00

we'd be knocked over by all the young lads

that'll be grand

too late altogether, sure the day is nearly gone away from us

what business would i have going in that late?

oh haha, i'm not going 'nightclubbing' at all haha

X: - straight in A: - That one goes all over the place

S: - I don't know what way it is at all on Sundays

BHM: - Let me see now, oh Monday is a Bank Holiday, I suppose that'll be like a Sunday

12

Fierce Hi-Tech

Do you know something, I find it easier to
understand the Mystery of the Blessed Trinity than
some of the gadgets that are going now.

In our own good time

Young people who are 'knacky at this sort of thing' talk about the Theory of Diffusion of Innovations. This theory says that for an idea or technology to spread or diffuse through the population it must be accepted by five different categories of consumer: Innovators, Early Adopters, Early Majority, Late Majority and Laggards. While there are Irish Mammies scattered throughout these groups, a

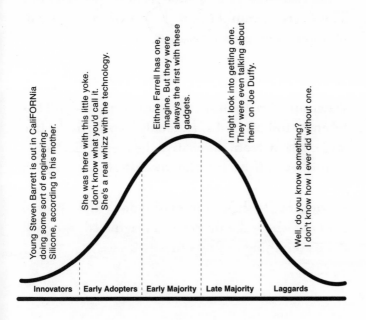

Young Steven Barrett is out in CaliFORNia doing some sort of engineering. Silicone, according to his mother.

She was there with this little yoke. I don't know what you'd call it. She's a real whizz with the technology.

Eithne Farrell has one, 'magine. But they were always the first with these gadgets.

I might look into getting one. They were even talking about them on Joe Duffy.

Well, do you know something? I don't know how I ever did without one.

| Innovators | Early Adopters | Early Majority | Late Majority | Laggards |

goodly proportion would quite often be towards the latter end of the adoption cycle – not because they are unable to deal with the technology, but because they don't need it or the technology just doesn't suit yet.

Upwardly mobile

Of all the small, fiddly yokes to be invented in the twentieth century, the mobile phone has surely come closest to 100 per cent market penetration. There are a number of points to note about Mammies and phones.

1. A missed call is a major event

Watch an Irish Mammy, for whom time and toil has taken its toll on limbs, suddenly leap vertically like an impala up from the chair at the merest electronic sound, even if it's just the low-battery warning on someone else's phone.

For those Irish Mammies who don't know how to find out where the missed call originated, they will drop everything to find out who it was.

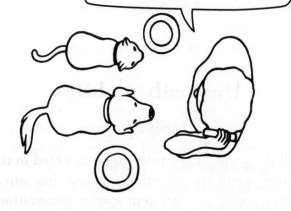

2. The learning curve is steep

Chuckling at Mammies' texting foibles is a popular sport. Consider what it's like for older Irish Mammies who never used computers before and never learned to place their blind trust in semiconductors, motherboards and bits and bytes floating through the air. This was a generation who never 'deleted' or 'cancelled' or used the arrow key to get the 'cursor' — whatever that is — in the right place to insert a missing word. Instead, they crossed things out, or started again on a new sheet of paper and saved the first attempt for use as a shopping list. Missing words were put in with '^'.

Texting was never an easy concept to master.

Understanding the principle of pressing a small button to get the right letter doesn't come naturally. The unnerving 'Just trust it, it knows what you want to say' experience of predictive texting can be problematic even for younger generations, jujing by d wey dey txt.

Once the basics of texting are mastered, the final frontier is punctuation.

There is limited room on a keypad for extra buttons, but one large one with a full stop would have been helpful. There's no point in hiding it behind the 1 and a symbol that's a cross between a scroll and a hair-roller. The result of this is that some texts from Mammy will consist of a number of unrelated ideas coalesced together in a stream-of-consciousness paragraph of which Joyce would be proud.

3. But Mammies are up to the task

Mammies are nothing if not resourceful. Aware of the limitations of digital communication, they have developed their own ways of correcting errors. For example, if an Irish Mammy forgets a word in the middle of a sentence, she may put the missing word at the end of the sentence, along with an explanation of where the missing word should go.

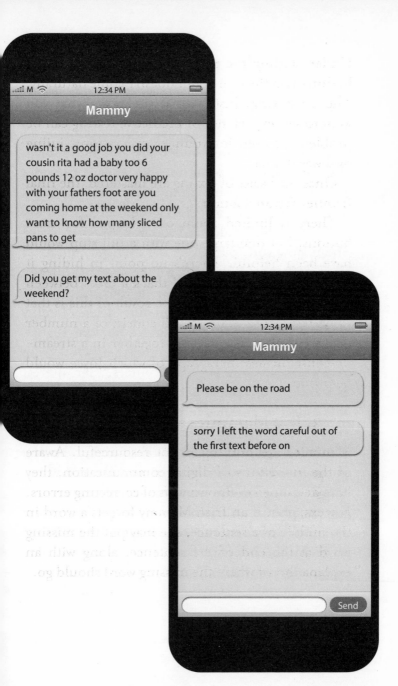

A tangled web

And then there's the Internet — its adoption by all Irish Mammies is well under way; but its complete diffusion has only been possible when it provides information an Irish Mammy really and truly wants and that she cannot get anywhere else. The key driver for this could be Facebook. Waxing lyrical about how you found out the average rainfall of Tegucigalpa on Wikipedia will be greeted with the same faint interest she shows in your other non-core activities. Say to a 'non-line' Irish Mammy that the Internet is convenient for booking flights, and she'll say 'Isn't that great altogether? God, ye're real whizz kids now at the computers.' Her interest is a little more piqued, but she is content to let this aspect of commerce pass her by for now. But if you are able to tell her exactly who was at Deirdre Mullane's wedding at the local church, who she got married to, what the dress was like and where they're going on the honeymoon, all because you saw the photos on Facebook, an Irish Mammy will say: 'Ah, there's no two ways about it now, I'll have to get on the Internet. Sure, I'm missing out on a whole other world.'

This is the canals-to-railways moment — one mode of communication is falling into disuse, so it's time to move the freight a different way.

When the transformation is complete, the world will be a very different place.

Indian summary

With Irish Mammy open to the Internet, a new type of challenge is presented:

(*Phone rings*)

Mammy:
There's the phone — *in the name of God*, who would be ringing now, and we in the middle of *Coronation Street* … (*picks up phone*) Hello?

Rajesh:
Hello, my name is Rajesh. I am calling from TechTech Support Solutions Limited.

Mammy:
Oh yes? Rajesh, is it? That's not an Irish name anyway — where are you at all?

Rajesh:

I am calling from our support centre here
in Bangalore. We are calling because ...

Mammy:

Bangalore! Isn't that a good one? Would
you believe, a cousin of mine has a
daughter working in computers, and she'd
be out there a lot. Would you have come
across her, I wonder. Catherine McGowan?

Rajesh:

There are 8 million people in Bangalore.
Please, if we could just look at your
computer ...

Mammy:

And, you know, Catherine was saying it can
get very hot out there. Forty-five degrees,
she said. What's it like there now?

Rajesh:

Now it is a little cooler but, please, we must
talk about your computer. We have detected
a virus, and ...

Mammy:

A virus! On the laptop? You know, my
youngest girl bought it for me, I've hardly
used it, except the ...

Rajesh (*interrupting*):
Are you near your computer? Can I ask you to just open it up?

Mammy:
Wait a minute now till I get my glasses …

(*Mammy disappears and is gone for five minutes*)

Mammy:
OK now, sorry, Rajesh, they're never there when you'd be looking for them. I have the computer, and what was it you wanted me to do?

Rajesh:
Press the Windows key.

Mammy:
Which one is that? Is it the one with the flag on it?

Rajesh:
Flag? What flag? … oh yes, of course, yes, that's the right one. Now, if you could just press that …

Mammy:
OK so. I pressed it.

Rajesh:
And what do you see?

Mammy:
Nothing.

Rajesh:
Nothing?

Mammy:
No, the screen is still black. Well, you never
said to turn it on.

Rajesh:
*I think you are making a fool of me. You talk about a
girl I should know in Bangalore and tell me it is hot in
my city and now you like to waste my time. You are a
#¿%¡$^! Goodbye.

Mammy:
Oh, the Lord save us.

Rajesh would have saved himself a lot of time if he'd
rung the Irish Mammy next door.

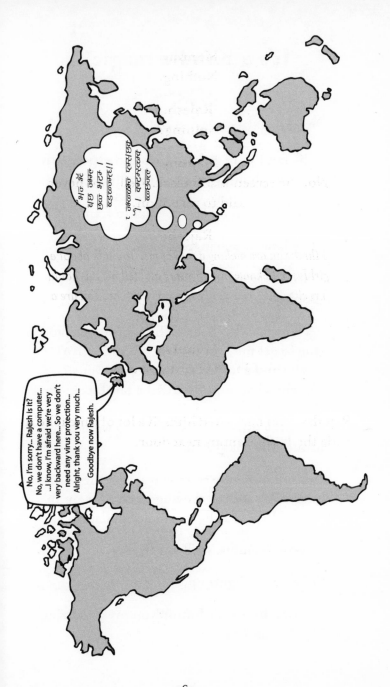

It's a Kindle magic

'And this is from all of us.'

The family are gathered around expectantly as Irish Mammy unwraps the slim present.

'Oh, it's … a … kind of a photo frame, is it?'

The family exchange glances.

'No, Mammy, it's a Kindle. It's for reading books.'

'A Kindle. Oh, haha, I thought ye were going to get me a *candle*. Oh, a Kindle. Isn't that wonderful? Well, thank you ever so much. That must have cost a fair bit. I know how scarce money is these days, and ye all running two cars. A small thing would have done. But thank you.'

It's not quite the ecstatic reaction they were expecting and, as she hugs each of them in turn, there is a slight sense of deflation.

'Look, Mammy, we'll switch it on.'

The screen lights up.

'Look, there's the button you press to bring up the options.'

'Options. I see,' says Mammy, weighing up her own options for getting away from the Kindle and its eerie glow.

'See, Mammy,' says one of the Family, taking it from her.

'We've put a couple of books on it for you. That's Nuala O'Faolain's book. Remember, you were saying that you wanted to read her book?'

'Oh, poor Nuala O'Faolain, the cratur. I've always had a soft spot for her. A great woman altogether. She had a hard life indeed.'

She's silent for a minute, pondering what Nuala would have made of Kindles.

'How would I go about getting these books for this then? Would they have them in Easons?'

She chooses her words carefully, remembering the guffaws when she asked them a few Christmases ago where would she get film for a digital camera.

'Well, you could go into Easons, or you could download them.'

'I see of course, yes. Down Load them. Right.'

There is a pause. The family have stopped talking, so Irish Mammy seizes her chance.

'Anyway, I'm going to put on the vegetables now, so I'll put that Kindle somewhere safe, for fear 'twould get dirt on it.'

The Kindle is put away in the same location as some other improving presents that have yet to be used. The typical pattern for such a present is that it is inquired about roughly once a month. And there it might lie until one day:

'Hello, Mammy, any news for me?'

'Well, I was going to ring you indeed! Didn't I get another eBook, isn't that what you call them … eBook? Yes, well didn't I get an eBook Down Loaded on to the Kindle?'

Adult Child hears these strange words from Mammy's mouth and wonders if she's speaking in tongues.

'How did you manage that?'

'Well, I'll tell you now. Isn't there a lovely young fella in the town after opening up a bookshop, and I went in there, you know, just to give him a bit of business. I told him about the Kindle and said I didn't know how to get a book. "Well," he said, "I'll Down Load them for you." So when I heard that,

"Right," says I, "I'll do this now once and for all." I brought the Kindle in with me the next time I was there, and yer man plugged it into some sort of I-don't-what-you'd-call-it. Then, says he, 'It's Down Loaded now." Cool as you like. And wouldn't take any money for it, *high nor dry*.'

'What book did you get?'

'I got Joe Duffy's autobiography.'

13

Roadworthy

Well, one thing he was always good at — finding
the way to places.

B ehind every great woman is a man who knows
his place. But Himself is useful in other areas.
One of those areas is The Road, and an important
aspect of this is The Salute.

The rules of the road

Visitors to Ireland often remark on how strangers
driving past will wave to them. They are so charmed
by this that they may not realize there is a complex
etiquette behind The Salute. First, they need to
understand the mechanics.

The position of your hand on a steering wheel,
giving maximum control, is one of the first things
to learn in a driving lesson. Ten to two, ten to two
— the mantra was repeated by or to all of us at some
stage during those first stressful miles on the road.
We know now of course that it is perfectly possible
to control the steering wheel with one elbow on the
ledge of the window and an idle finger on the wheel,
the other hand occupied with fags/sangwidge/bag-
a-Tayto wedged between our legs.

The real reason for ten to two is this. On a country road, it is the optimum hand position from which to launch the forefingered salute. This is the all-purpose gesture acknowledging the presence on the road of another human being. The gesture is designed to allow minimal expense of effort. This ensures the fingerer against the humiliation of not getting a response. In the countryside, it is best to give the one-fingered salute to everyone you meet. (Not to be confused with the 'other' one-fingered salute.)

Whatever the salute, the other road user or pedestrian should respond in kind.

If Himself knows the other person, the one-finger salute is swiftly upgraded to a full arm wave and a mouthing of the other's name.

Saluting reaches its peak ebullience if both involved are commonly agreed to be Characters.

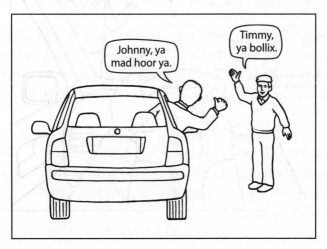

Himself and other Himselves

Himself may encounter other Himselves gathered in conversation on the road.

It is appropriate to address them indirectly, asking a question about their well-being without necessarily implicating yourself in any concern:

'How're the men?'

And by identifying them straight away as men, it allows them to speak as men do when talking about themselves – either peremptorily or not at all.

> 'Dhera, not too bad, Johnny.'
>
> 'Not a bad day for it.'
>
> 'No indeed. Not a bad day for it at all.'

The use of 'it' could, in theory, refer to any outdoor activity but, strictly speaking, should be confined to some sort of physical job taking place on the side of the road: clipping a hedge, clearing a blocked drain, painting a gate and – the epitome of roadside activities – building a dry-stone wall.

Like the corncrake, the 'not a bad day for it' is under severe threat from modern industrial and agricultural methods. Very little work is done now on the side of the road that doesn't consist of just a man in a digger.

For years, county councils used to send a man

out to patrol the sides of the road with a bicycle, a shovel and his dog. He fixed 99 per cent of roadside issues. Now, they do nothing, and wait until the 99 per cent problems have coalesced – in the way the Occupy Movement could only dream of – to form a Giant 1 per cent problem. It is only after being shamed by a report on the news when a local blames the council's inaction for the bridge collapse that the council now has to send three diggers and a team of men – where one man, a shovel and his dog would have sufficed.

The group of men stand there now, having ascertained that they are all 'not too bad at all'. They agree the weather is suitable for 'it', and they are in danger of running out of things to say when they are assailed by a loud beeping. A hairy forearm waves out the rolled-down driver's window as the car flies past. Everyone gives the big salute – the size inversely proportional to the certainty of who it was in the car.

'Who was that?'

'Barry Twomey. Murty Twomey's boy.'

'What's he doing?'

'Working away on the bypass over. He's a stonemason.'

'Isn't that a nice little number he's driving?'

'Oh, shur — it's a licence to print money over there.'

'A mighty job.'

Himself is mad about roads — seeing roads widen, taking the corners off them, bypasses. Not for him the bucolic charm of tootling along green, narrow, winding lanes.

Roads and stories of mighty roads are strong currency in conversation about faraway places.

'You had a good time over?'

'I did.'

'Fierce roads they have, don't they?'

'Oh, don't be talking-to-me? Even the road in from the airport in Chicargo. Eight lanes on it.'

Even when Himself is not driving the vehicle, the roads fascinate him. Especially on the odd night Himself is the Man Who Wanted to Talk to the Bus Driver.

This is a man that you never see in an advertisement for Bulmers' Irish Cider. Those ads are as an unrealistic portrayal as you will see. There is no crowd of people with good skin and hair congregating in a marquee on the edge of an orchard. The true image of rural drinking is a man in his fifties getting on the late bus at closing time and chatting loudly to the driver about that 'bad bastard of a bend' and in general about 'the hoor of a road'.

Not that the bus driver cares one jot for the hooriness of the route or the parentage of the bends, but he listens politely as the man in the front passenger seat gives his views on bus-driving and road design.

If *The Lord of the Rings* had been set in Ireland, at some stage the intrepid hobbits would have needed directions....

> Sam looked up towards the orc-tower. Frodo stirred uneasily in his sleep. Sam needed to find a way through to Mordor. Then he noticed a man in a flat cap and Penneys jumper looking at him.
>
> 'Can you tell us a way through here?' asked Sam hesitantly.
>
> 'How far did ye come?'
>
> 'We have travelled from the Shire.'
>
> 'What way did ye take?'
>
> 'We have travelled through the Old Forest and Emyn Muil and we lost a good friend at the Bridge of Khazad Dum.'
>
> 'Ye needn't have come that way at all – there's a grand new road there now. The whole thing is bypassed.'

A roundabout way

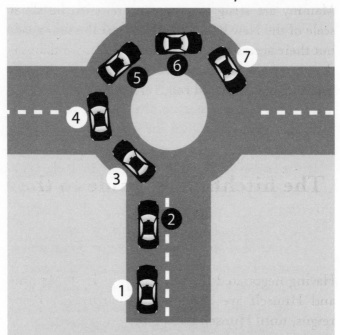

1. Take care here now, Sean, for fear you'd miss the turn-off.

2. I know. Indeed we missed it before.

3. Slow down now. It's left. Left. LEFT!

4. **Ah you've it passed now.**

5. **LEFT?**

6. But we never went left there before.

7. Well you go left there now according to the signs. Because of the new bypass I suppose.

Despite this love of the roads, both Himself and Irish Mammy are struggling to comprehend the sheer scale of the New Roads. And not just the new roads but their accessories — slip roads and roundabouts that litter the countryside. They are increasingly unavoidable as the old roads are closed off.

The hitchhikers' guide to the parish

Having negotiated the roundabout, Irish Mammy and Himself are back on familiar roads. Peace reigns, until Himself takes unilateral action.

> 'I'd better stop and give this fella a lift.'

> 'Ah don't, you wouldn't know what he'd be like.'

As very few people hitchhike now, the ones that do definitely have a story. Sometimes it's a broken-down car, but more often than not it's the kind of story that a journalist in search of a 'human interest' piece would extract from a man queuing at a social welfare office.

True to form, when the car stops and the door opens, the hitchhiker sits in, stubbly and possibly the worse for drink.

> 'Thanks very much indeed. Fair play to ye for stopping.'

> 'Ah, no problem at all,' says Himself.

Irish Mammy is a little uneasy with a strange man sitting behind her. Ordinarily, this would be a perfect opportunity to pump this man for information on the locals, to get up-to-date news on births, deaths, marriages and who's 'gone from the Homeplace and somewhere back along the road with a Welshman', but she holds back. She thinks, a little sniffily, that this fella wouldn't move in enough circles to pick up tidbits, but she is wrong. This man is a pub-man and, sooner or later, all parish news goes through the nexus of the pub.

Himself sees a quiet journey ahead, so breaks the silence.

> 'Are you going far?' asks Himself into the rear-view mirror.

> 'Anywhere at all along the road. I'm going to Sammy's Bar.'

Of course, thinks Mammy, and on a Monday morning too.

'Is that place still open?' says Himself, addressing the 500lb elephant in the car but not acknowledging that it's taking up any room.

''Tis. There's a new manager there now. A Polish fella be the name of Tadeusz. He's making a mighty fist of it. 'Tis full every night with music and all that craic.'

'A Polish fella?'

'Yeah – he's married to Kathleen Lyons.'

Mammy's ears prick up. Married? Obviously, he moves in enough circles to pick some bit of news. And she recognizes the name Kathleen Lyons. Like the sultan idly contemplating what to do with the life of a prisoner, she decides that perhaps this man may be of some use. And she speaks up for the first time.

'Kathleen Lyons got married?'

'Oh, she did. A huge wedding too. Someone said there were three hundred and fifty at it.'

'*Three hundred and fifty*,' says Mammy, imagining the horror. 'That's an awful size for a wedding. The Polish fella must be doing well.'

'Oh 'twas Jimmy Lyons paid for the whole lot. The father.'

More information!, thinks Mammy.

This stool pigeon is singing like a canary.

'Where did Jimmy get that kind of money?'

'Oh shur, he sold a farm over in Kilfeedan. The one he got from th'aunt. Got big money from some developer. 'Tis NAMA have it now I'd say.'

The stories are now flying from the back of the car to the front like a *Sky News* ticker. All Irish Mammy has to do is ask the right questions.

'Janey mac! And were you at the wedding?'

'I was, yes. Arra, me and Tom Lyons'd be good enough friends like. I used to drive a truck for him a while back. Steve O'Brien is my name.'

'Are *you* Steve *O'Brien*?'

'The very same.'

'Well, I didn't recognize you at *all*. I suppose I haven't laid eyes on you in twenty years.'

The spell is broken. She 'has him placed

now' and visibly relaxes. The hitchhiker, for his part, moves into the centre of the back seat to address them both, and they both eagerly lap at the fountain of gossip, including the bad news that they'd missed at least two funerals.

'We didn't even *know* about it. You see, we only get the paper on Sundays.'

14

The Big Match

No, there's no mass. The whole lot'll be done in the hotel. I didn't say anything of course. Although I'd love to know what his parents think of this.

To paraphrase Shakespeare: 'All the world's a wedding, and all the men and women in it merely guests' — guests who 'act up' from time to time.

With more than 20,000 weddings in Ireland every year, that's a lot of guests and a lot of potential for acting up. With the world of dates, venues, bands, suppliers, families and (unfortunately, yes) Irish Mammies closing in around them (mainly), brides need somewhere to go to vent. More often than not, they go to the online wedding forum.

Up for discussion

The sheer amount of opinion and advice on wedding discussion forums is astounding. One of the more popular sites in Ireland has more than 1.5 million opinions on 160,000 subjects.

BlushingBride23	**Re: What to put in the basket in the toilets**
Posts: 560 Joined: Mon May 07, 2012 7:17 am	OMG Definitely tights. If one of the girls got a ladder and I didn't do anything about it, I'd feel I let them down.

Like any community, these forums have their own language and abbreviations. CBM is not a leading provider of IT solutions for today's challenging environment — it's the Chief Bridesmaid. CBMs can be saints or sinners. They comfort a stressed bride but are also the engineers behind hen-party events that were not part of the bride's express wishes.

FSILs are not investment products designed to secure your financial safety in your retirement — it's a future sister-in-law, who quite often proves to be a crucial intermediary and passer-on of important information to the FMIL — the future Mammy-in-law.

The forums reveal as much about the key players' personalities as about the minutiae of organizing the event. The Irish Mammy — be she a FMIL or a MOB — does not get a good press. In many discussions, fairly or unfairly she is portrayed as a mysterious figure in the background. She is seen pulling the strings, subverting the democratic decisions of the spouses-to-be, working for her own nefarious purposes, possibly because of deeply held beliefs about 'the right way to do things'.

When a blushing B2B is not getting the requisite support from her OH (other half) or H2B (husband-to-be; not a pencil), the blame is laid squarely at the door of his upbringing by his Mammy, who excessively doted on him.

More often than not, the intervention of the bride's mother, or FMIL, is direct and, in a situation where tensions are already high, it can spark a full-blown conflagration over things like:

• The colour of the Irish Mammy's dress

Love2LoveU	FMIL REKKING MY HEAD!!!!!!!!!!
Posts: 980 Joined: Mon Feb 07, 2011 10:20 am	hiya girls need to vent !!!!! Just spoke wit my FMIL about colours of outfits an I asked her wat colour she was wearing and she goes IVORY!!!!! OMG My WEDING dress Is IVORY!!! ,Am I being stupid about this?

• Or the invitations

PrettyInPink	Need 2 vent. Going to explode!!!!!!!!
Posts: 225 Joined: Thu Oct 20, 2011 3:12 pm	Ladies help me!! FMIL invited a load of randomers to the wedding

RE:Need 2 vent. Going to explode!!!!!!!!

AAARRR!! Listen to this ladies. I hear from his sister yesterday that her mam went out and bought a packetof shite INVITATIONS IN TESCOS!!!! I think she wants to send her own out if we don't give her ours

In this atmosphere, all clues are seized upon as a sign of subterfuge.

What's going on here? These Mammies are sane and rational women who over the years had 'a million and one things to do', 'didn't know *where* the week went to', 'were in and out to the Eye, Ear and Throat with the youngest', but still managed to get all they needed to get done done. Yet, around wedding time, some are consistently accused of 'acting like it's their Big Day'.

They're not — they just want different things. For the average Irish Mammy, the wedding of a child is like a stressful combination of a stockmarket Initial Public Offering, a family reunion and having the neighbours around for dinner. Rightly or wrongly, Mammies may feel the whole world is watching. And, what's worse, they don't have control over everything, and this can be expressed in some odd behaviour, like making secret trips to the Venue to sample the food, in case it was 'too unusual for the likes of Mrs Dooley'.

Mammy-in-law

The forums can only prepare you so much. Eventually, you will have to run the gauntlet — particularly, if you are a future daughter-in-law.

The first meeting between a prospective partner/spouse and an Irish Mammy can be daunting, especially if she is the Mammy of a son. But don't worry unduly. The bond is overplayed. She's not going to be spending the whole day muttering darkly into her tea towel *à la* Mammy in the Kerrygold advertisement.

If dinner is at Irish Mammy's place, eat everything — forego lactose, fructose and glucose intolerances for one painful IBS-laden afternoon. (Unless you're risking anaphylactic shock brought on by nut allergy. But don't worry — you won't be getting nuts anyway.)

The plates and the food *are hot enough* full stop. If they are zero degrees Kelvin and entropy is tending to its minimum value, as far as you are concerned, the plates are hot enough. If they come out of the oven glowing and burn a hole in the table, Irish Mammy will still worry they've gone cold. Your job is to reassure her. It's probably futile, but don't make matters worse.

Do not be surprised if your future Irish Mammy-in-law hugs you. She may be so relieved to see him bring home anyone, joy will be unconfined. This could equally apply if her son is gay and bringing home his 'partner'. No matter how much she may pronounce the word *partner* in italics, she is delighted. A second gay man in her life is a blessing more and more Irish Mammies are learning to love. She has been dying *for years* to meet one of her child's *partners*. And she knows this will be very juicy news for the relatives, so Irish Mammy will be very excited indeed.

There will be something around the house that Irish Mammy regrets was not cleaned/mended/replaced in time for the visit. Don't mention it unless she brings it up first: 'I suppose you must think us very backward, Sasha, with our old-fashioned oil-burning stove.' Reply immediately with 'No, Mrs Gould — quite the opposite. I remember we had exactly the same one. They're mighty yokes all the same.' It doesn't matter if you were brought up in a refugee camp in Darfur or a brownstone house in Westchester County — empathize.

Manners Manners Manners Manners Manners Manners. Mammies notice manners more than anything else. Display good manners on your first trip, and your reputation is cemented for life. On your return, you could lead her son in on a dog collar while thrashing him with a wet towel and throwing yoghurt at the wall. You will still be regarded as mannerly — 'if a little unusual'.

Irish Mammy may list off her son's failings to

you in detail – this is not a trap. Just smile and say, 'Oh now, he is all right' or, better still, 'I know, I'm working on that one myself.' Mammies love to collaborate on projects, and this project – her son – is being handed over to you.

Make an attempt to help with the dishes. You will be rebuffed. Insist once and then back down.

It is likely that her son will not have the nerve to discuss the living arrangements in the house you are clearly sharing. Avoid phrases like 'Well, when Anthony and I were looking for a bed it was important the springs were really durable' until you know the lie – in every sense of the word – of the land.

Differing approaches

There's no doubt about it – things have changed since Mammy got married. The upcoming nuptials have set Mammy and Himself to reminiscing.

> 'Of course it was called a wedding breakfast then, and it was Donie's brother brought us to the church in an old Ford Anglia.'

> ''Twas a Prefect actually.'

'Well, a Prefect, or whatever it was. And I remember our priest arrived on a bicycle. A bit of a character for the times that were in it. He had a big head of long hair. He looked like one of the Rolling Stones or something. Honestly.'

'A grand singer.'

'He was. But it's different now. There's so much more to think about now. Wait till I tell you what Aine showed me on her computer. A "mood board" she calls it.'

'"A mood board?"'

'Yes. Says she, "It's for inspiration."'

'Inspiration – what does she want that for?'

With so much inspiration flying around in the lead-up to the wedding, it's little wonder that Mammy and the fiancé(e)s start to diverge on a number of details.

The differences are often crystallized first on the wedding invitation:

**FI &
HALLERS
ARE GETTING
HITCHED!**

**JOIN US AT OUR
WEDDING FESTIVAL**

**2PM AUGUST 9TH 2014
CIRCUS TENT, HILL OF TARA**

**OLLOWED BY HOG ROAST, DRINKS,
DANCING & A MACNAS PARADE**

**DETAILS ON OUR BLOG
WWW.SMOOCH2014.COM**

*Mr and Mrs Sean Callaghan
request the pleasure of the company of*

Mr and Mrs Padraig Hayes

At the wedding of their daughter

*Fiona
to Dr Gerard Hallissey*

*At St Fachtna's Parish Church,
On Saturday August 9th 2014 2pm*

*and afterwards at the
River Castle Lodge Country House Hotel
for beef, salmon and a waltz.*

Once the invitations are designed, the melting
wax and the envelopes designed to evoke Edwardian
grace have been bought, there follows another
challenge: who to invite.

Negotiations on the guest list will often start
in a very civilized way but, as the weeks progress,
'someone' is going to have to have words with 'a
certain parent'.

It all started out fine ...

From: Fiona Callaghan <fi-fi-trix1980@gmail.com> Date: Fri,
Jun 15, 2012 at 8:50 AM
Subject: Invitations
To: Theresa Callaghan <theresacallaghan1950@eircom.net>

Hi Mammy, Hope you are well. Have you and Daddy
thought about who you want to ask to the wedding from the
neighbours? Space is very tight in the teepee so if you can only
limit it to a few. I'd say eight MAX.
Looking forward to seeing you on Saturday. I'm sure you'll
find something in McCarrigals. They have a great selection for
MOBs (Mothers of the Bride!).
Love Fi X

But there was a surprise in store ...

From: Fiona Callaghan <fi-fi-trix1980@gmail.com>
Date: Fri, Jun 15, 2012 at 10:00 AM
Subject: FW: Invitations
To: Gerard Hallissey <hallersledge@gmail.com>

Hi, hun,
See below. OMG!!!!!!!!!!!
Xxx
ps Help!
---------- Forwarded message ----------

Mammy had some surprise guests.

From: Theresa Callaghan <theresacallaghan1950@eircom.net>
Date: Fri, Jun 15, 2012 at 9:30 AM
Subject: Re: Invitations
To: Fiona Callaghan <fi-fi-trix1980@gmail.com>

Dear Fiona,

Thank you for your email. I was laughing at being called an
MOB. I'll be like Tony Soprano or something. I suppose I'll have
to learn all the lingo now.

I'm sure you must be very busy with everything so I'll keep this
short. Here's the names of the people we'd like to invite.

The Donnellans – your father would have a lot of business with them.

Mrs Caulfield in Rosscarn. She was always very good to you.

Mr and Mrs Dynan and maybe a slot for Gary because they
won't have anyone to mind him.

The Pattersons. They'll hardly go but they'd like to be asked all
the same.

Bill Sisk and I suppose if you ask him you'll have to ask the rest
of them. I think there's three or four of them.

Dan the Hat – You'll never hear the end of it if he's not there.

Sally Sweeney and her mother. Nose was very out of joint when
she wasn't asked to your brother's, so I can't show my face at
cards if we leave her out again.

Some representation from the football. Maybe set aside two or
three for that.

And then all the cousins on Daddy's mother's side. We were at
most of their weddings.

Philly Clancy and the family and the Byrnes of course.

And Doctor Costello.

I'll ask your father to see whether he's any more to add, but
that'll do for starters anyway.

We'll see you on Saturday anyway P.G.

I hope they'll have something to fit me now in this boutique.

Love
Mammy

Parent trap

At some stage, the Mammies-in-law-to-be will meet for the first time. One has to feel for them. They will enter into a relationship which they will hopefully have to maintain for the rest of their lives. Within a few weeks, they'll be in-laws. Whether they like it or not.

The start of every relationship has its hopes and fears. But for couples in love, they do have a certain amount of control over it. The transition from glassy-eyed stare in a crowded pub to lifelong commitment is full of small, incremental steps. But spare a thought for the parents. They've no choice as to who they get as in-laws.

It's like a generation-reversed arranged marriage:

> 'Mothers, fathers, my fiancée and I have been discussing this and now that we are getting married we've arranged that you are all to become friends.'

One can only imagine how much of a strain these meetings must be, though, when one side is at a completely different social level. For example, if you happened to be hanging around Rome in the early 1500s and started doing a steady line with a woman called Lucrezia Borgia, then you were storing up one hell of a tense lunch for your parents.

Lucrezia was in fact the daughter of the Pope. If your son was marrying Pope Alexander VI's daughter, it's fair to say the suit you wore to the GAA dinner dance would not do. You would also be well served learning every version of grace before meals you could find (including the old, harsh version which said that you must gouge out your neighbour's eye if he didn't eat his broccoli). And no matter how well prepared you were, it would still be a very fraught experience. How would you engage in small talk?

> **Pope:** So Finbarr, Lucrezia tells me you work in insurance. How's business?
>
> **Finbarr:** Ah, not too bad, Your Holiness. Busy enough now, although this latest Plague has put the kibosh on a lot of things, you know. But sure we'll struggle on, I suppose. And yourself, how are things going for you?
>
> **Pope:** I'm the Pope — so things are going pretty well.

Also, it would probably be best to let the Pope lead the questioning, lest you say something you shouldn't.

> **Noreen:** And how about your lady wife, your Eminence, will she be joining us?

Pope: (*silent stony papal glare*)

Noreen (*blushing*): ... I mean, like ... em ...
These new potatoes are lovely altogether.
They're like balls of flour.

Looking further back in history, to antiquity, there
are many florid accounts of epic love stories, but
usually the narrative lacks the essential ingredient
of the drama, when the hero and heroine's parents
meet for the first time.

The story of Helen of Troy has fascinated
historians throughout the ages, but there is no
account of what happened when Paris's parents,
Priam and Hecuba, met Helen's mother and father,
Leda and Zeus, leader of the Greek gods.

Priam and Hecuba were themselves no slouches,
being the king and queen of Troy, but even so,
they must have been on tenterhooks. If talking
to the Pope would be hard, imagine talking to a
fully fledged god. Expressing even the mildest
of complaints about the weather could lead to a
bolt of lightning zinging its way across the table.
Alternative topics would need to be chosen:

Hecuba (*smiling nervously*): So, Leda, tell me
how did you two meet?

Leda: Oh, this fella. He's such a charmer.
He landed in my yard, disguised as a swan.

One thing led to another …

Hecuba (*blushing*): Oh … right. There's a grand stretch in the evenings these days, isn't there?

Zeus: I did that.

15

A Bit of Culture

Would you believe that last time I went was *Michael Collins*. That'll tell you now.

While the Irish Mammy features as a character in many different fields and genres of the Arts, often she is not the central one. This chapter tries to reimagine some iconic works if Irish Mammy was allowed to assume her rightful place at the centre of matters.

Films

2001: YOU'RE GOING WHERE? WHAT DO YOU MEAN, 'SPACE'?

Two astronauts on a highly advanced spaceship are on a mission to Jupiter to investigate signals that appear to emanate from a mysterious black monolith. Unfortunately, they reckon without the intervention of the ship's hugely powerful on-board computer, the Mammy 9000.

Dave:
Open the doors, MAMMY.

Mammy 9000:
I can't do that, Dave.

Dave:
What's the problem?

Mammy 9000:

Are you mad, child? If I opened that door,
I'd let in such a draught that'd nearly give
you double pneumonia.

Dave:
I won't argue with you any more! Open the
doors!

Mammy 9000 (*almost to herself*):
What's the matter with him now at all? He's
gone very cranky.

Dave:
I am *not getting cranky.*

Mammy 9000 (*as if ignoring him*):
Overtired, I'd say.

SCENE ENDS

Star Wars V: There'll be no striking back.
The empire's had enough excitement now for one day

Luke infiltrates the Death Star with the hope of killing Darth Vader and freeing his friends from persecution. Unfortunately, before he can fulfil his destiny, he encounters his real mother.

Darth Mammy:

Luke, listen to me now. Are you listening to me? (*to herself*) He's not listening to me at all. Come over here now!

Luke:

I'll never join you!

Darth Mammy:

Luke. Will you put down the light sabre for a minute? You'll have someone's eye out with it.

Luke:

No! No!

Darth Mammy:

Luke! I'm your mother and I'm telling you to put it away. You can play with it again later.

SCENE ENDS

Books

An Irish teenage vampire novel

The teenage vampire novel has been wildly successful, but strangely, few have been set in Ireland. This is about to be put right.

This is the story of a young girl, Ella, on the cusp of womanhood, who is irresistibly drawn to the magnetically attractive Eddie Callinan. But Eddie is a vampire! Can their love ever prosper? This excerpt should whet the appetite.

'Ella, peitin, are you getting up or what? You told me to call you in plenty of time – now would you get up like a good girl? Your father is anxious to get the papers before Mass. Honestly, it's like trying to wake the dead here.'

I stirred drowsily. My mother's words were far away. I could still see him. His face as he held it close to mine. Eddie. The translucent skin, the coal-black eyes piercing into my soul, and then the expression of revulsion. What had caused that? Did he want to shift me or not?

'Ella! I'm not going to call you again. Get up!'

Eddie Callinan disappeared and I, reluctantly, awkwardly, roused myself from my bed. When I came downstairs, my mother was waiting with a curious expression on her face.

'What time did you get in last night?'

I mumbled through a mouthful of porridge, 'About eleven?'

'Oh, it was later than that. It was after 12 anyway.'

When we entered the church, my mother did not go to her usual place but walked down the aisle, directly to where the Callinans were, and motioned me to go in. I was going to be sitting next to him!

'How are you, Doctor Callinan?' my mother whispered loudly along the pew, past me and Eddie. 'Cold enough out –' she followed up.

''Tis', Bernie,' said Doctor Callinan. 'The nights are closing in,' he added meaningfully.

'They are indeed, and how are they all at home?'

'Oh they're grand, not a bother.'

'This boy is Eddie, is it?'

''Tis.'

'He's gone so grown-up. Eddie and Ella are in the same class in school.'

'That's right.'

I looked down at my lap, hot with shame. During Mass, I could hardly remember the responses, I was in so much of a haze. I could feel Eddie glaring at me – those coal-black eyes burrowing deep inside me. He never said a word and, when it came to the 'Peace be with you' he took my hand coldly, though his grip was strong from his muscular, alabaster forearms.

As we walked back to the car, my mother was bursting with conversation.

'He seems like a nice young lad, and of course his father is a great doctor. I remember when you were small you had an awful temperature. I went up first to Doctor Garvey, but he was useless. '"Tis only a cold," says he – "give her a Lemsip."

'Well, I wouldn't take no for an answer. I knew something was wrong, so I went up to Doctor

Callinan. He took one look at you, and says, "She has Blood Poisoning – take her straight up to the hospital." He's an expert on blood, apparently. A great doctor altogether, and as young-looking. I wouldn't say he's aged much in the 20 years we've been around here. Of course, they're all vampires, the Callinans, but shur we have to move with the times. And, to give them their due, they still go to Mass. They're a lot more devout than the so-called Catholics around here, I don't mind telling you. I have my eye on young Eddie for you.'

My mind was in turmoil. How could I have any wordless, months-long, locked-in-my-room angst about Eddie if my mother approved of him? I would be better off with a werewolf.

Oh, it's one of *those* books

Who could have believed that, after the vampire phenomenon, it would be a book of fan fiction based on flagellation and bondage that would singlehandedly – pardon the turn of phrase – boost the flagging publishing industry?

He moves towards me now – graceful yet powerful like a tiger stalking an antelope.

My own excitement is palpable. The air between us becomes a force field of lustful charge. Any move now could set off the sparks between us as if we were both knives in a microwave.

'You know The Rules,' he says.

'I know The Rules,' I say, enjoying the game.

He moves closer. The anticipation is almost more than I can bear but I know we must take it nice and slow.

There is a tremor in his voice as he says, 'We'd better be quick now because Mammy'll be home soon from devotions.'

Fifty Shades of Mammy

C P O'Regan
#1 Ireland's Own Bestseller

DO YOU FEEL UNFULFILLED IN YOUR JOB?

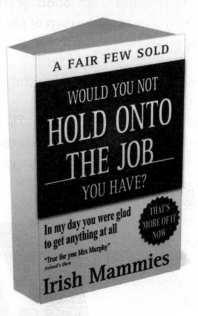

Do you get the sense that you have not made the progress in your career that your talent and work ethic deserve?

By examining the habits of the most sensible people in the world, Irish Mammies help you in a step-by-step way to come to the conclusion that, for goodness' sake, keep hold of that job. Especially these days. Ah, don't mind your oul job satisfaction. You could be a lot worse off. You could be in Somalia or somewhere.

The Tea Towel of Mammy

Colm O'Regan

Do the deep questions of the world keep you awake at night? Have you ever wondered why? Well, I'll tell you now, it'd be more in your line to do what your mother asked you to do the first time and don't mind your whining about it.

These words of wisdom will sustain you, and that should do you grand. Similar to *The Tao of Pooh* or *The Te of Piglet*, *The Tea Towel of Mammy* is the multivitamin for the soul.

Existentialism
That's the why

Living in the present
Now–Now

Buddhism
You're not hungry at all.
You just think you are.

Mindfulness
Mind!

The book also contains haiku. The haiku is a form of short poem originating in Japan. Its beauty is in its brevity and the juxtaposition of two complementary yet separate images or ideas. Themes of nature are quite common. In haiku, there are three lines of five, seven and five syllables respectively.

Reproduced overleaf — with kind permission of the author — is a haiku meditation to take you through the year.

January
'Oh Yes … Yes … Go 'way! …'
That was Kate Carr. The school's closed
On account of snow.

                       February
               And put Science down
               It's a handy one. You can
               Change your mind after.

March
I suppose they'll be
Maith-go-leor around the road.
Badly off they are.

                          April
               Blustery rain, cold.
               Global warming, how are ye?
               Nearly May. 'Magine.

May
Have you any cap?
For goodness' sake, wear a cap.
It's not summer yet.

                            June
               Would you credit it,
       As soon as they get their hols,
               The oul weather breaks.

July
Do you know something?
I think you got a small bit
Of colour today.

August
Ah what about it?
I'll patch the elbows on it.
It'll do you grand.

September
Wait a minute now,
You need *another* workbook?
'Twasn't on the List.

October
Once the clocks go back
The days are knackered. We'll be
By the fire tonight.

November
Which reminds me now
I must get the envelope
For the Holy Souls.

December
And would you believe,
Didn't I forget mixed peel?
I'll have to go back.

Theatre

If only ... Hamlet's mother was Irish

Shakespeare's *Hamlet* is one of the great works of literature of the last millennium. One of its strongest themes is the relationship between Hamlet and his mother. This relationship becomes more fraught as Hamlet grapples with his own prevarication, the machinations of others at court, the realpolitik of his uncle and, of course, the appearance of a ghost. Hamlet could have surmounted all of this, had his mother been far firmer with him when he was 'acting the maggot'.

An Irish Mammy would have put a stop to this nonsense straight away.

THE
Tragicall Historie of
HAMLET,

Prince of Denmarke.

By William Shakespeare.

Hamlet   To be Or Not To be
That is the question
Whether it is nobler ...

Gertrude   HAMLET!!!

What are you doing up there. Are you
talking with yourself again?! I thought I
told you you'd go mad doing that?

Hamlet   I'll drive you mad now in a second.

Gertrude   What was that?

Hamlet   Nothing Mother. I am coming down now.

12 Angry Mammies

You couldn't be up to them.

Mammy has always taken an interest in the happenings of the world. She has, for example, been acutely aware of each humanitarian crisis to hit the world's poor. And, by extension, so have her children, when it was used as a reason to stop their whining. Generations have grown up feeling guilty about complaining when there are children in Biafra, India, Ethiopia, Somalia, Darfur and North Korea that are far worse off.

But now, with her own country in dire straits, it's time for Mammy to rule. It's tempting to imagine how different things might have been if governments had been led by Mammy in the past.

If only Irish Mammies were in charge of the tribunals

There have been a number of tribunals set up in Ireland to look into wrongdoing in high places. They have taken years and cost millions. A healthy scattering of Irish Mammies asking the hard questions could have saved the country time and money.

Tribunal Chairman:
I now call upon Senior Counsel for the State, Ms. Irish Mammy, to put questions to the witness.

Irish Mammy:
What in the name of God were you at at all?
Was it horseplay or what?

Witness:
I'm … afraid … that question is out of order.

Irish Mammy:
You'll be out of order now, when I get you home. I'll redden your arse out of order if you don't give me a straight answer. Did you take money from that developer?

Witness:
I … I … this is preposterous.

Irish Mammy:
Don't mind your preposterous. Tell the truth and shame the devil.

Witness:
I have nothing to hide. I have told the truth all the way through this tribunal.

Irish Mammy:
You have in your eye. You can't fool me now, mister. Don't forget I was changing your nappy before you knew anything about rezoning and the rest of your smartness.

Witness:

(*silence*)

Irish Mammy:
Have you nothing to say for yourself?

Witness:

(*silence*)

Irish Mammy:
I can ring the developer's mother as well too, and find out from her ...

Witness:
I didn't do anything, I swear.

Irish Mammy:

(*taking out phone*)

Well then, she'll confirm that. I'm ringing her.

Witness:
Fine.

Irish Mammy:

One last chance, and if I find you were lying to me … Well let's just say I'll be *very* disappointed in you.

Witness:

(*pauses; then, sniffing*)

Stop! Stop! Don't ring, OK, I'll tell you everything.

Irish Mammy:

That's the boy. Tell Mammy everything.

Witness (*sobbing loudly*):
Ididn'twanttodoitbut … (*gulps*) everyone was doing it.

Irish Mammy:

And I suppose if everyone was jumping off a cliff you'd want to do that too. But at least you're telling me. Now, I'm not angry with you. Who else was involved? Was it that Charlie fella, did he start it?

Mammy and the bail-out

Our negotiating teams over the last few years have been overwhelmingly male. Maybe the ECB thought they were dealing with the boss. But they were wrong.

Epilogue

We'll see.

As Ireland continues to change, there is the understandable fear that the Irish Mammy we know and cherish will change irrevocably, that something precious will be lost. But we forget about her resilience and adaptability. Even though the future may be a strange country full of lasers and hovercars and everyone wearing aluminium-foil onesies and teleporting around the place, the Irish Mammy will survive.

She is a product of her culture, her environment and the regular threat of rain. What's more, in the coming years, there will be a new type of Irish Mammy. In the next 50 years, even new Irish women who did not have an Irish Mammy themselves may become one, almost by osmosis.

At this stage, you may well be asking yourself if you are turning into an Irish Mammy. There will come a moment when some phrase or sentence escapes your lips and as the words float through the air, you clap your hand to your mouth in sudden realization: 'I think I'm turning into my mother.'

To prepare you for that metamorphosis, on the next page are some of the stages of progression, from here to Mammyternity.

	Stage 1	Stage 2	Stage 3	Stage 4	Stage 5
Socializing	Can we get Taytos, please pleaseplease pleaseplease?	OMIGOD OMIGOD Mum's outside. Can you smell it off my breath?	Blitzed last night.	I don't know when was the last time I was out.	We haven't a spare minute with Aoife's wedding, and your father's ear.
Spins and Lifts	Can you bring me to piano, Mammy?	Look just drop us here – we'll walk the rest of the way.	He failed me on 'Progress'. What does that even mean?	I should put taxi plates on the roof the amount of toing and froing I'm doing.	The roads are all changed here since the bypass. You'd want your wits about you.
Coats	I'm fine, Mammy. I don't need any coat.	I'm totally taking it off when she drops us outside.	I think I must have left it in a taxi.	Put on your coat for goodness sake. Do you want to get pneumonia?	Do you know something, I'd be lost only for this coat.
In the Media	Could I say to my teacher Mrs Downey and .... everyonewho-knowsme.	It would mean so much to get through to Bootcamp.	I don't know Ray. He just looked too 'random' so I switched off my light.	I'm a mother myself, Joe.	I never protested before, Pat, but this was just the final straw.
Himself	Nooo I don't like him. Stoppittt.	OMIGOD OMIGOD Doyouthinkhesaw melookingathim?	Apparently he doesn't do 'commitment'.	I do.	Ah, he's not the worst of them.

The future of the Irish Mammy is safe – and if she is safe, so are we.

Glossary

Acting up: Opportunistic bad behaviour by children in the presence of a visitor. It is done in the hope that they will be placated by a treat. However, if the behaviour has been diagnosed as acting up, it is less likely that it will be appeased. Further incidents may be referred to simply as 'more of it'. *See also* **More of it**

A good one: A coincidence or chance meeting. The coincidence chiefly relates to relations.

'And it turns out wasn't she the same Cathy Buggy that was a first cousin of Kieran Buggy who used to teach you the tin whistle. Isn't *that a good one?*'

Aired: A bed that has been treated with radiator, electric blanket and general worrying for a period of seven days prior to being slept in by a visitor or returning child. *See also* **Damp**

Damp: Any item of clothing, or something capable of being sat or slept on, that has not achieved the sort of dryness one would expect from a Dead Sea Scroll kept in a sealed jar in a desert cave. *See also* **Aired**

Deedn'I: Abbreviated form of 'Indeed, I', but used to emphasize that the Mammy has very definitely not taken a course of action promulgated by legislators or the more vulgar aspects of society.

    '*Deedn'I* did not get any spray tan.'

Fostuch/Luadramán: Children, usually male, who are at home watching telly when they should be:

- Out in the fresh air on a grand day like today.

- Getting up to let their father sit down there, it's his seat.

- Helping their mother around the place. They're *well* able.

Horseplay/trick-acting/hi-jinks: The chief cause of an unfortunate event, according to the intuition of an Irish Mammy.

    'How in the name of God did they manage to break that toilet? You may be sure there was *horseplay* involved.

Hot press: The spiritual core of the house. A small cubbyhole containing a large hot-water cylinder.

If you don't mind: An ending to the sentence, indicating surprise that the subject has achieved a certain goal.

'Sandra Nolan has set up her own business — beauty treatments and massages, *if you don't mind*. Isn't she an enterprising little thing all the same?'

Latchico: Himself would use this term to identify general fecklessness or uselessness in an unspecified individual.

'Plenty of *latchicoes* idle enough around the place to pick up the rubbish, but you won't see them do that at all.'

'Magine: Short for 'Imagine'. An exclamatory statement to emphasize a statement about a neighbour whose child is further away than Irish Mammy had previously thought.

'Dubai?!! 'Magine that.'

More of it: A further instance of behaviour proving an earlier held maxim that overall behaviour — of a five-year-old child, the family, society in general — is on the decline.

Musha/Wisha: Filler words that are used in sentences that express doubt or the rejection of a course of action.

'*Musha*, they wouldn't have much interest in me for their MRBI poll, I'd say.'

'*Wisha*, we won't be bothered watching them oul Oscars. We'll see it on the news tomorrow anyway.'

'Nawful Cold: The kind of cold one would get from sleeping in an unaired, damp bed. Should an Irish Mammy inflict this on a visitor, she may never forgive herself. *See also* **Aired; Damp**

Quare: Odd, strange. It is *not* a pejorative term for a gay man. Often, there is nowt as *quare* as straight folk. (Note that *quare* can also mean 'very', though there is no recorded instance of anyone being 'quare quare'.)

Safe Place: Where the lost thing is. It is so safe it cannot be accessed by wind/rain/mice/Irish Mammy. *See also* **St Anthony**

Socializing: Refers to a broad swathe of night-time activity, ranging from a courtesy call to an elderly relative to embarking on a drug-fuelled odyssey along the Reeperbahn that culminates in an *Eyes Wide Shut*-style fetish party. *See also* **Horseplay/trick-acting/hi-jink**s

St Anthony: The saint who hides something secondary and not as important as the primary lost object so that Irish Mammy will find the main lost object while looking for the secondary. Then St Anthony places the secondary object on top of the table. *See also* **Safe Place**

You needn't: It is better for the sake of cohesion or privacy within the family/community that you do not impart what Irish Mammy has just told you.

'*You needn't* bother telling your sister about that now.'

About the Author

Colm O'Regan is a critically acclaimed stand-up comedian, columnist and broadcaster. He writes a weekly column for the *Cork News* and has written for the *Irish Times* and *BBC Online Magazine*. Colm is a regular contributor on Irish radio and on the BBC World Service. As a stand-up comedian, he has performed to sell-out crowds all over the world from Tokyo to Cape Town and including the Edinburgh Fringe, the Cat Laughs and the Montreal Just For Laughs Festival. His stand-up has also featured on RTÉ's *Late Late Show* and on Comedy Central. From Dripsey in County Cork, Colm now lives in Dublin (but he'll ring home on a Sunday evening for news).

Acknowledgements

Thanks to Brian, Eoin, Phil and all at Transworld for getting excited about this book from the start, striking the write and right tone in all their editing, advice and encouragement.

Thanks to Faith – who was true to her name – and all at the Lisa Richards Agency for their invaluable support and advice.

Thanks to Doug, whose illustrations captured the 'look' of an Irish Mammy perfectly. Thanks to Nick Avery for your patience in laying out a book full of fiddly bits.

For my wife Marie, for her love, bestfriendship and support not just in this but in all my quixotic endeavours over the last few years.

Finally, for my mother and father who between them inspired at least some of the book but who also inspire me in myriad ways that couldn't be stored in just one 'funny book'.

Finally, finally, to @irishmammies's 50,000+ followers on Twitter who with their good nature and good humour made a Mammy feel fierce proud altogether.

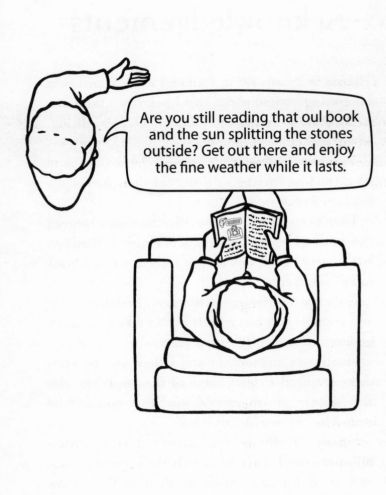

Are you bringing us from the church to the reception?

Now

Don't lose that now
whatEVER you do.

There's the rain now.

Will one of y
down th

And she wouldn't be the st

Are you going with me this evening or will you go with
your father to the 11 o'clock?

I've the e
tonight. '
Glob

Wait'll you see now, as soon as they get their
holidays, the weather'll break.

And will there be
supervision at this . . .
disco?

I can't sit the exam for you.

He'll fall off that wall.

Stop that now, d
it or I'll ta

Bread soda! I KNEW
I forgot something.

You'l

You put on a bit of weight since the last time you
were down. No harm.

Could I have te
wonder would y

There's a fine solid-looking girl.

Lookit.

Well, scrape off the burnt bits so.

A day for the

You're watching the match
are you? I thought I heard
some language alright.

Thanks! It was reduced.

Is that
alread

Who are you meeting in town tonight, is there any
harm in asking? . . . Oh I'm glad. Mairéad has her
head screwed on at least.

Wh

That cup is too near the edge there.

I can't tomorrow peitín. I'm defrosting the freezer.